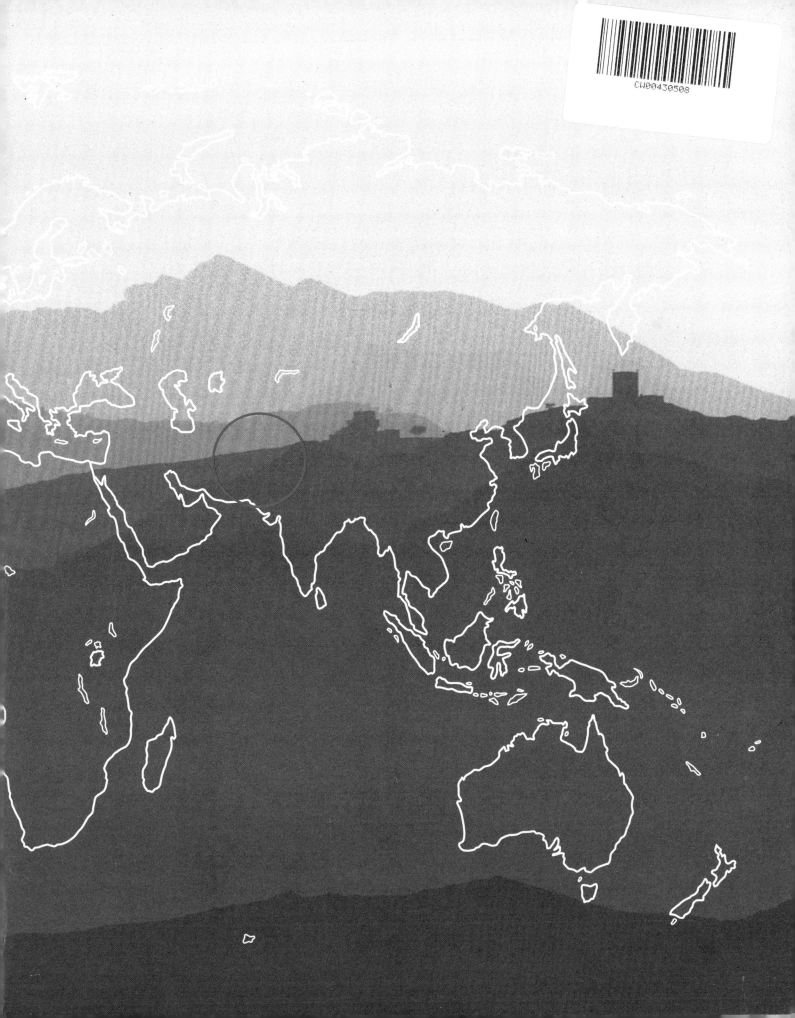

Cover: A grizzled elder of the Mohmand tribe wears the customary cotton turban twisted over a basketweave skullcap. In the background photograph, the evening sun gleams on a river flowing down from his homeland—the forbidding hills of the North-West Frontier.

Front end-paper: The circle drawn on this outline map of the world indicates the location of the Pathans' rugged territory amid the arid mountain ranges that straddle the border between Pakistan and Afghanistan. The Mohmand Pathans described in this volume live in the North-West Frontier Province of Pakistan.

Peoples of the Wild Series

This volume is one in a series that undertakes to record the unique lifestyles of remote peoples who have not yet yielded to the encroaching pressures of the modern world.

PEOPLES OF THE WILD
THE EPIC OF FLIGHT
THE SEAFARERS
WORLD WAR II
THE GOOD COOK
THE TIME-LIFE ENCYCLOPAEDIA
OF GARDENING
HUMAN BEHAVIOUR
THE GREAT CITIES
THE ART OF SEWING
THE OLD WEST
THE WORLD'S WILD PLACES
THE EMERGENCE OF MAN
LIFE LIBRARY OF PHOTOGRAPHY
THIS FABULOUS CENTURY
TIME-LIFE LIBRARY OF ART
FOODS OF THE WORLD
GREAT AGES OF MAN
LIFE SCIENCE LIBRARY
LIFE NATURE LIBRARY
YOUNG READERS LIBRARY
LIFE WORLD LIBRARY
THE TIME-LIFE BOOK OF BOATING
TECHNIQUES OF PHOTOGRAPHY
LIFE AT WAR
LIFE GOES TO THE MOVIES
BEST OF LIFE

Guardians
of the North-West Frontier
The Pathans

by André Singer
and the Editors of Time-Life Books
Photographs by Toby Molenaar and Michael Freeman

PEOPLES OF THE WILD · TIME-LIFE BOOKS · AMSTERDAM

TIME-LIFE BOOKS

European Editor: Kit van Tulleken
Design Director: Louis Klein
Photography Director: Pamela Marke
Chief of Research: Vanessa Kramer
Chief Sub-Editor: Ilse Gray

PEOPLES OF THE WILD
Series Editor: Gillian Boucher
Head Researcher: Jackie Matthews
Picture Editor: Jeanne Griffiths
Series Designer: Rick Bowring
Series Co-ordinator: Belinda Stewart Cox

Editorial Staff for *Guardians of the North-West Frontier*
Text Editor: Alan Lothian
Staff Writers: Louise Earwaker, Deborah Thompson
Researcher: Deirdre McGarry
Designer: Zaki Elia
Sub-Editor: Charles Boyle
Proofreader: Judith Heaton
Design Assistant: Paul Reeves

Editorial Production
Chief: Ellen Brush
Quality Control: Douglas Whitworth
Traffic Co-ordinators: Linda Mallett, Helen Whitehorn
Picture Co-ordinator: Philip Garner
Art Department: Julia West
Editorial Department: Theresa John, Debra Lelliott, Rebecca Read,
Sylvia Osborne

Published by Time-Life Books B.V., Ottho Heldringstraat 5, 1066 AZ Amsterdam.

ISBN 7054 0702 0

TIME-LIFE is a trademark of Time Incorporated U.S.A.

Contents

The Author
André Singer, who has a doctorate in Social Anthropology from Oxford University, has been a Vice President of the Royal Society for Asian Affairs, the editor of several books on anthropology and the author of numerous articles on Central Asia. He made his first expedition to that area in 1967, and has spent several years living among tribal groups in Iran, Afghanistan and Pakistan. He has also been involved in several ethnographic films for the British television documentary series, *Disappearing World*.

The Photographers
Toby Molenaar, a freelance photographer, has travelled widely in Europe, Africa, North and South America, and the Middle and Far East, working on assignments for most of the major European and American magazines as well as for Time-Life Books. Born in Holland and educated in Switzerland, she has exhibited her work at several one-woman shows.

Michael Freeman began his photographic career after studying geography at Oxford University. His photographs have appeared in many magazines and books, among them two Time-Life Books series: *The World's Wild Places* and *The Great Cities*. He is also the author of a number of books on photography, including *The 35 mm Handbook*.

The Volume Consultant
Dr. Akbar S. Ahmed, a Fellow of the Royal Anthropological Institute in London, was educated in Abbottabad, Pakistan, and at the Universities of Cambridge and London in England. He has published several books on Pathan society. Among the senior positions he has held in Pakistan's Civil Service are those of Political Agent in the Orakzai and South Waziristan Agencies of the North-West Frontier Province. In 1981, he was a visiting professor at Harvard University in the United States.

The Series Consultant
Malcolm McLeod, Keeper of Ethnography at the British Museum, was born in Edinburgh. After studying History and Social Anthropology at Oxford, he undertook research in Africa, concentrating on the Asante region and other areas of Ghana. He has taught in the Sociology Department of the University of Ghana and at Cambridge, and is the author of a book on the Asante.

Introduction

High in the mountainous borderlands of Pakistan and Afghanistan lives one of the most warlike peoples on earth. For centuries, the Pathans have survived by force of arms, fighting outsiders and each other for every inch of their rocky territory. They live by a code that knows no compromise: feuds can last for generations and a man's honour is held to be more important than life itself. Their women are kept hidden from the outside world and any violation of this system of purdah is punishable by death.

No external power has ever ruled the Pathans. In recognition of their stubborn independence, the government of Pakistan has designated 40,000 square miles of land as "tribal territories" in which national laws have no force. There, the Pathans live much as they always have done—relying nowadays on herding and agriculture instead of banditry, but maintaining as fiercely as ever their ancient ethos.

When Time-Life Books made plans to send a writer and a photographer into this proud, closed society, it was of paramount importance to find in advance a community that would accept the strangers when they arrived. Consultant Dr. Akbar Ahmed recommended that the book focus on the Mohmand village of Kado, where he himself had studied and made many acquaintances. Thus it was that one of Kado's senior families took in the Time-Life team—and became the book's most prominent characters.

Choosing the team was trickier than selecting the location. Because of the rules of purdah, it was clear that any outsider would be precluded by his or her gender from observing both the male and female roles in Pathan society. The eventual solution involved two separate expeditions. First, author André Singer and photographer Toby Molenaar were sent to Kado village. As a woman, Toby was given some photographic access to the daily life of females inside a Pathan household and was able to brief Singer about it, thus rounding out his first-hand experience of the male side. Later, photographer Michael Freeman was sent to the same locale charged with paying special pictorial attention to the ways of tribal manhood.

Although the team members inevitably felt some trepidation upon entering the territory of the warrior people, their anxieties were soon quieted. The granting of hospitality to those who seek protection is as central to the Pathan code as blood revenge against those who threaten their honour. Writer and photographers alike not only were made welcome in Kado, they became firm friends with their generous hosts.

The Editors

One | A Warrior Heritage

By dawn, after a climb of one hour, we had reached the hilltop a thousand feet above our starting place in Kado village, itself more than a thousand feet above sea level. My three armed guides squatted on the rocky ground, looking cool and unruffled despite our arduous climb and the steadily increasing heat of early summer. I gasped for air as discreetly as possible and wiped my face with a sweat-soaked handkerchief. My hosts had brought me to this commanding height to show me their homeland in the early daylight that spilled over the landscape. We were in the heart of Pakistan's North-West Frontier Province, a chaos of mountains where the Indian subcontinent shoulders its way into Central Asia. My companions were Pathans, men of the hill tribes that for centuries have jealously guarded this hard land from all intruders. I followed the tribesmen's gaze eastward, looking across the great plain of Peshawar to the distant horizon, where the sun edged into the cloudless sky. To the north and west loomed a succession of barren ridges that looked bleak and forbidding despite the rosy flush of morning.

Shams-ud Din, the oldest and most senior of the three Pathans, pointed away from the rising sun to the south-west, where more peaks glowed pink. At their base, clusters of mud-walled houses were emerging from mist and darkness. Shams-ud Din spoke: "Over there you can see Kaja Ghundai, the crooked peak. That is in the land of the Afridi Pathans. On the other side of the peak lies the Khyber Pass and our friends the Shinwaris." The Pathans are divided into about 50 distinct—and often mutually antagonistic—tribes. My hosts were Mohmand Pathans; in stressing that the Shinwari Pathans were his friends, Shams-ud Din was strongly implying that the Afridis were his enemies. He did not dwell on the subject, however, but continued with his geography lesson. "Behind us is Afghanistan. Most of the land in that direction is empty; we use it only for grazing our sheep and cattle, for hunting rabbits and wild goats, or to hide in during times of trouble." Then he pointed down towards the plain, where the many tributaries of the Kabul river glis-

tened in the early morning light. He indicated two of the nearer seasonal streams, or *khwars*. "Our land lies between the Kado Khwar and the Rawal Khwar. All who live there are related: we are the Kado Khel, the clan of Kado. Further south is the Kabul river itself, near the fort at Michni. Beyond that are the settled lands, and the city of Peshawar."

It was from Peshawar that I had come to Kado, across the line that divides the Pathan tribal territory from the rest of Pakistan. The squat Michni fort, a relic from the days of the British Empire, was only one of a chain of outposts that stretches along the 400-mile length of the tribal lands—an armed border that aptly symbolizes the unique status of the Pathans and indicates the degree of independence they have been able to retain. The nation of Pakistan has a strong central government, yet more than three million Pathans, occupying an area of 25,000 square miles on a strategic frontier, remain their own masters. Across the border in neighbouring Afghanistan, almost four million Pathans share the same way of life. Together, they constitute the world's largest tribal society—a total of at least seven million people who still order their affairs by the law of Islam and by the rules of *pukhtunwali*—"the Way of the Pathan"—a harsh, uncompromising code that requires blood vengeance for insult and values honour above life itself. For more than 2,000 years, the hill tribes have defended their independence and way of life with the stubborn ferocity that *pukhtunwali* demands.

The geographical position of the Pathans' homeland has ensured plenty of fighting. The mountains I could see in a towering arc around the plain of Peshawar are part of an unbroken chain that runs more than 800 miles from the deserts of Baluchistan in the south to the 20,000-foot peaks of the Hindu Kush in the north. For much of that distance, the mountains divide Pakistan from Afghanistan; in the far north, the Hindu Kush merges with the Pamirs, where China, Afghanistan and the Soviet Union share an icy frontier. The extent of the mountain barrier gives great strategic importance to the few passes that cut through it; they are the only gateways by which armies could cross from the Asian land mass to the riches of India.

The troops of Alexander the Great passed through the region in the fourth century B.C., and Greek historians recorded the tenacity with which the *Paktue*, as they called the hill tribes, defended their homes. Succeeding waves of invasion followed Alexander. In medieval times, tribes very similar to present-day Pathans stood off the Mongol hordes of Genghis Khan. In the 16th century, the Moguls under the emperor Babur descended from Central Asia to establish dominion over all India. All India, that is, except the North-West Frontier: the Mogul Empire lasted 200 years, but it was never able to bring the Pathans under its control.

In those days, the tribesmen were generally known as "Afghans"; the name Pathan was brought into use by the British, India's next rulers. The British adopted the term—pronounced "Pa-taan"—from a Hindu corruption of the word *Pakhtana*, meaning speakers of the Eastern Iranian language of Pukhtu or Pushtu. To this day, the Pathans still call themselves Pukhtuns or Pushtuns, depending on which of the two main dialects they speak.

Not even the British Empire, at the zenith of its power in the 19th century, could impose its concept of law and order on the hill tribes—or even stop their raids on the settled lowlands around Peshawar and beyond. The failure was not due to lack of effort. The British regarded India as the jewel of their Empire, and saw the North-West Frontier as its most vulnerable facet. There were two threats. The first came from the Pathans themselves, who for centuries had lived by raiding and extorting tolls from the caravans of mules and camels, laden with all the goods of Asia, that used the mountain passes. Imperial administrators found such behaviour irksome, to say the least. But the second menace was the more serious. Throughout the 19th century, Tsarist Russia had been expanding into Central Asia. One people after another was devoured by the "Russian Bear", until only Afghanistan and the Pathan tribes remained as buffers between the two great powers. The ensuing intrigues, manipulations and conflicts were aptly called "the Great Game" by British statesmen. The stakes were high: the British were determined to protect India by controlling the area between them and their Russian rivals, and the "game" led them to three bloody wars with Afghanistan and countless skirmishes with the Pathans, involving considerable loss of life on both sides. After one five-month campaign against the Mohmands in 1897, the British admitted to 1,150 casualties; they did not count the Pathan dead.

The British used tactics similar to those of the Moguls before them: at regular intervals, they sent powerful forces into Pathan territory to cow the tribes by sheer might. But supply was always difficult in such rough, largely roadless terrain; after a month or two, the alien troops inevitably had to withdraw. Punitive expeditions usually accomplished little. The Pathans simply retreated into their arid hills. From these natural fortresses, they watched their villages burn, licked their wounds and waited for a chance to strike back in their own way: an ambush sprung on an isolated column, an outpost massacred in a sudden night attack, an unwary sentry with his throat cut.

In Kado village, in the tribal territory of the Mohmand Pathans,
10-foot-high mud walls surround households. The walls afford
security against attackers—and privacy for the tribe's womenfolk.
In addition to housing, each compound includes structures for
storage and animal shelter. The trees in the courtyards provide
cooling shade in the frequent 100°F temperatures of summer.

The British, like their predecessors, eventually realized that it would be easier to placate the tribes than to fight them. A line was drawn round tribal territory. The tribes enclosed by it were allowed to manage their own affairs in return for access along the main routes leading through the mountains and for "good behaviour". The British, for their part, granted aid in the form of money and irrigation projects. By "good behaviour", the British meant that the Pathans were not to raid the people in the settled areas; there was to be no large-scale warfare between the various tribes; caravans were to be allowed to travel the roads without being held ransom, and there was to be no more insurrection against the British Empire.

The system helped stem the fighting but never stopped it altogether. In 1873, the fort of Michni, near Shams-ud Din's village of Kado, was attacked and its commandant killed. In the 1880s, the Mohmands alone launched more than a hundred raids against the British, stealing gold, cattle and women from the Hindu population of the plains. The favoured retaliation for such breaches of the agreement were fines against the whole tribe, collected at bayonet point if necessary, destruction of the culprits' villages and reprisal raids that confiscated goods and weapons. These crude methods did nothing to foster affection between the Pathans and their "masters". As recently as 1930, a well-organized Pathan raiding party almost succeeded in storming the city of Peshawar; and in 1935, the British were so stung by Mohmand depredations that they marched a heavily armed force more than 30,000 strong into the tribal areas to exact punishment for Pathan misdeeds.

The three men with me, silhouetted with their rifles against the jagged sky-line, could have been waiting to take part in one of these skirmishes—and I, as an Englishman, would have been at the receiving end of their rifles. But British rule had ended in 1947, when Pakistan achieved independence; since then, the Frontier has seen no open warfare. Far from being the enemy of the Pathans, I was their guest. I had come to their land to learn about their way of life, and I already knew that the violent code of *pukhtunwali* had another side: a strict law of hospitality that no tribesman would infringe.

I had first met Shams-ud Din only a few days before, in the city of Peshawar, the ancient capital of the Frontier Province. Photographer Toby Molenaar and I were arranging the final details of our expedition with Dr. Akbar Ahmed, an anthropologist who was also a Pakistan Government political agent for the tribal territories. "The journey you will be making is not a long one in terms of miles," Dr. Ahmed explained, "but it will take you beyond the effective reach of my government. No one really rules the Pathans. The government influences by negotiation, not by force. We build roads, we help with irrigation schemes and we try to keep the peace. But our laws are not enforced in the tribal territories. I can arrange for you a permission that will allow you through the police check-point into the Mohmand area, but you will need more than that once you have crossed over. If you want to visit the Mohmands, you must find a Mohmand who will accept responsibility for you. Such a thing, fortunately, is not impossible. I have a friend who lives in the Mohmand village of Kado, an elder named Shams-ud Din. I have spoken to him and he has agreed to offer you his hospitality and protection."

That was one major problem solved. But we had another difficulty. "How easily will they accept Toby?" I asked.

"Mrs. Molenaar will be treated with respect, of course," replied Dr. Ahmed. "In fact, they will probably treat her as an honorary man. Among themselves, they observe a very strict system of purdah. Women live for the most part in seclusion, and never appear unveiled before unrelated men. However, the system is not necessarily applied to outsiders."

"But in that case, will they allow her to live with their own women—and to photograph them?" We knew that if Toby achieved this objective, she would be the first Westerner to penetrate the high walls that literally, as well as figuratively, surround the lives of Pathan women.

Dr. Ahmed shrugged. "It cannot be guaranteed."

Our introduction to Shams-ud Din went well. He was a distinguished grey-bearded man, dressed in the white baggy trousers and long cotton shirt traditionally worn by tribesmen. With him was his son Ihsanullah, a handsome man in his middle twenties. They greeted Toby as they greeted Dr. Ahmed and myself, with a simple handshake. For the moment, at least, they were clearly treating her as a man. I was also relieved to discover that we would not have to rely on my few words of Pukhtu; Ihsanullah had learnt English at a school established by the Pakistan Government. Agreement was soon reached. The Mohmands had some business to accomplish in Peshawar and we would leave with them for Kado the next day.

We set off from Peshawar the following morning, heading north-west in a battered hired car driven by its grizzled Mohmand owner. In front of us a

Amid shellbursts and puffs of gunsmoke, faithfully rendered in this drawing for the Illustrated London News, Mohmand Pathans mount a fierce attack in 1897 on Shabkadar fort—one of several British garrisons on the North-West Frontier. After repulsing the assault, which cost the Pathans 300 casualties, Imperial troops were able for the first time to penetrate into the heart of Mohmand territory.

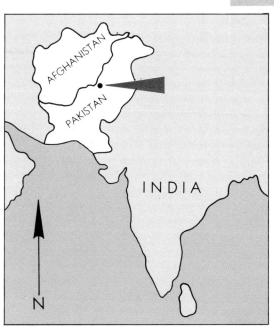

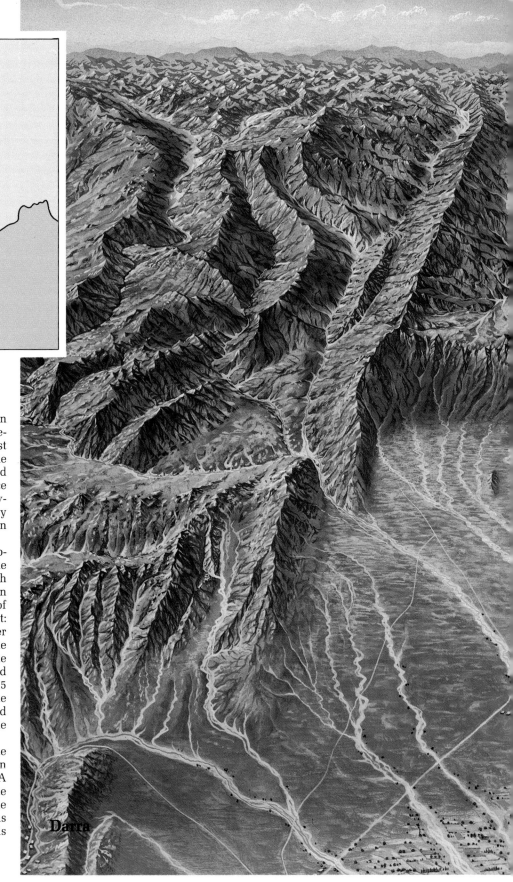

The Tribal Highlands

The barren mountains of the Pathan homeland sprawl along the frontier between Pakistan and Afghanistan. Most Pathan tribes live on both sides of the border. Many—including the Mohmand tribe—enjoy considerable independence in Pakistan's North-West Frontier Province, on a long stretch of tribal territory that is administered according to Pathan custom rather than by government law.

The arrow on the inset map locates approximately the village of Kado, the home of the Mohmand families with whom this book deals, and the direction of the arrow indicates the perspective of the large topographical map on the right: north-west along the line of the Khyber Pass and the Kabul river gorge. In the foreground of the latter map are the government-administered lowlands and the provincial capital of Peshawar, 15 miles from Kado. The boundary of the tribal territory skirts the plain; beyond are the mountainous tribal lands and the high plateau of Afghanistan.

Rainfall in the area is meagre; in the spring, however, melt-waters flow down from the snow covered mountains. A government dam at Warsak controls the once destructive floods and permits the cultivation of wheat, maize and barley as well as the sugar-cane that tinges this summertime view with green.

Darra

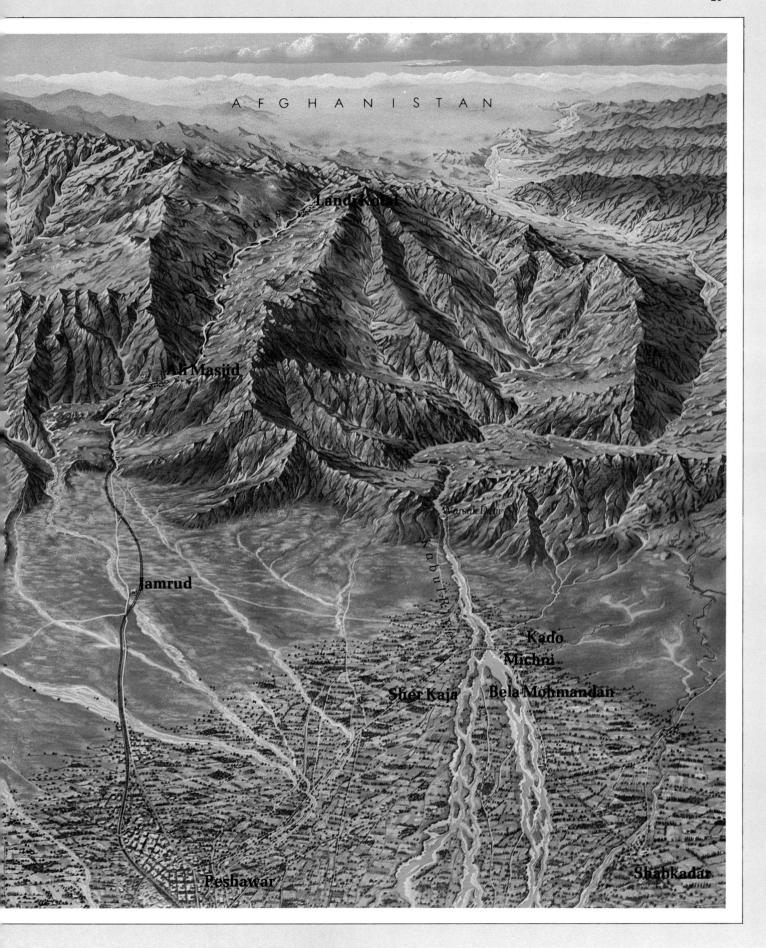

AFGHANISTAN

Landi Kotal

Ali Masjid

Jamrud

Warsak Dam

Kabul R.

Kado

Michni

Sher Kaja

Bela Mohmandan

Peshawar

Shabkadar

tarmac road stretched flat and unbending across the plain, disappearing in the distance where the Mohmand Hills rose from the hazy horizon.

For the first few miles, the traffic was heavy. We had to weave and honk our way past plodding water buffalo, loaded twice their size with sugar-cane, and herds of camels carrying crops and timber. Men in turbans of various colours—black, blue, yellow and white—walked alongside their beasts of burden; others in chattering groups waited by the roadside to crowd on to the vividly painted lorries and buses that served as local transport. Our pace, nevertheless, was brisk. Our driver obviously considered it a point of honour to miss anything that moved by as few inches as possible.

The surrounding plain was remarkably lush. Fields of wheat were turning from green to gold, and stretches of tall sugar-cane gave the region a near-tropical look. About 12 miles from Peshawar we had our first sight of the Kabul. We crossed the main stream and one of its many tributaries by way of a stone bridge, then swung off the road to follow a dirt track that led north-west towards the hills that rose on the river's far bank.

"Slow down," Shams-ud Din said to our driver. Moments later, we were halted by a chain strung across the road from two posts. In the bushes beside the road, we could see a dusty tent, and beyond that rose the squat towers of Michni fort. There was no sign of life.

"It is the police check-point," Ihsanullah explained. "It is controlled by the Frontier Constabulary." He grinned. "They are supposed to prevent any smuggling between the settled areas and the tribal lands."

We waited inside the car in the hot silence, Toby and I with a restlessness that contrasted markedly with the stoic calm of the Pathans. Eventually, a pair of large, army-issue sandals swung out from the nearby tent, followed by their owner—a uniformed policeman whose siesta had been disturbed. "Will he want to see our papers?" I asked Ihsanullah.

"I doubt it," he replied. "For one thing, it's too hot. And in any case, they all recognize my father. He is a respected elder and he can pass through when-ever he wants to go to his village." Ihsanullah was right. After only a cursory glance inside the car, the yawning soldier released the chain and waved us through. We were now inside tribal territory. By long-standing agreement, government control extended only to the main roads and a few forts. From this point on, our safety now rested on the goodwill of the tribesmen alone.

A few miles beyond the fort, we came to the fast-flowing Kado Khwar, one of the seasonal tributaries of the Kabul. Between the months of June and Sep-tember, it is possible to drive across the river-bed. This was late April, how-ever, and although the heat made it obvious that summer was well under way, melting snow from the mountains kept the river in flood. We had to say goodbye to our car and its driver, who returned along the dusty track to Michni. Crossing the 50-foot-wide river was only a matter of wading through the thigh-deep water, but Ihsanullah, guiding us across, slipped and got hopelessly soaked in the process, much to his father's amusement.

I had understood that we would have our first view of Kado village when we crossed the river. At first, I was disappointed. We had walked several hun-

Buoyed by an inflated goatskin bag, a strong tribesman kicks his way across the fast-flowing waters of one of the many snow-fed seasonal rivers that seam Pathan territory. The bag will retain its air approximately long enough for its owner to make the crossing.

dred yards, but all I could see were a few mud walls, about 10 feet high, and various paths that disappeared in different directions through tall sugarcane. "Where is the village?" I asked Ihsanullah.

"Why, here," he laughed. "This is Kado. It's all around you."

What had confused me was Kado's lack of an obvious centre. Walking on, I got a better view. The walls, in fact, were compounds and each compound was a dwelling. Some had corner towers and others seemed to be linked by communal walls in groups of two or three. At the base of each mud wall were a few layers of stones, which I assumed were some form of foundation. In fact, as Ihsanullah explained, the stones act as a damp course: they keep ground water from seeping up into the walls, thus ensuring that the mud remains dry and durable, and the gaps between the stones provide ventilation. But it was not the details of the buildings' construction that impressed me; it was their fortress-like appearance. With the corner towers and the massive double doors I saw in some of the walls, the effect was of a cluster of miniature medieval castles that lacked only drawbridges and moats.

"Are these high walls for defence?" I asked.

"Partly," Ihsanullah replied. "But also for purdah."

I did not pursue the question. I decided that, as a stranger and a guest in the village, it would be impolite, perhaps even dangerous, to inquire too deeply into a subject that involved the honour of Pathan womenfolk. That sensitive

Each arrayed with cartridge belt and rifle, turbanned men of Kado's senior family line up behind their patriarch, Shams-ud Din (seated, right), and his brother (left). The patriarch's eldest son, Ihsanullah, stands directly behind him, and bare-headed younger boys sitting at his feet hold two of his infant grandsons.

square, I could peer over the six-foot-high crenellated walls and see almost all of Kado spread out below to the north-east. In the background, towering above the village from the other side, was the hill of Ugda Tarakai where the villagers had once taken refuge from the British attackers. To the north were the mountains that dominate the entire region; from there, several days later, I was to have my first overall view of the frontier lands. South east was the view towards Michni fort and the Kabul river. On the south-west side of the tower, immediately below, were the mud houses and courtyards of families living in Old Kado. To avoid offending our hosts, I restrained myself from looking too closely in that direction.

It was late afternoon when we finally arrived back in new Kado. We found the scene almost unchanged. The elders were still lounging on their char-poys in the *hujra*, still idly gossiping; but now food was being brought out from the adjoining compound—chicken and eggs, flat leavened bread and an array of vegetables including spinach, onions, tomatoes and potatoes. By Pathan standards, this was a feast—bread and vegetables form a typical meal—and I recognized that it had been prepared specially for our benefit.

It was almost sunset when we finished the meal and, as night drew in, Ihsanullah invited Toby to leave the company of the men and to join his mother, wife and other women in the adjacent courtyard. We had hoped all along that this arrangement would be made, but it was with some trepidation that Toby said her farewells and disappeared behind one of the high mud walls to enter the hidden part of Pathan society.

Meanwhile, in the *hujra*, following the fifth and final prayer of the day—just after nightfall—several of the seven or eight remaining men wrapped them-selves from head to toe in a single sheet and, with rifles beside them, drifted off to sleep. Others continued talking in a desultory way.

I lay on my cot watching the fireflies until I could no longer distinguish them from the shooting stars. According to a Mohmand legend, a shooting star is a glimpse of an angel destroying a devil in the endless battle between good and evil. Each meteor meant one less devil to fight. As several devils fell towards earth, I wondered whether present-day Pathans lived up to their warrior image. From what I had already seen, it was clear that no Pathan male liked to be parted from his gun, but perhaps this was only a token of a bloody past: no more than a symbol, like those devils in the sky. Well, I would soon know. Meantime, I followed the example of my Pathan hosts and mummified myself for the night in a rough cotton sheet.

Brief, Carefree Days of Childhood

In childhood, Pathans enjoy a brief spell of freedom that stands in marked contrast to the strictly regulated lives of tribal adults. At puberty, the girls will be confined to the family compound and, from then on, the constraints of purdah close around them. For their part, the boys will have to uphold family honour according to the stringent Pathan code of manhood.

Before these milestones, however, they are given some tasks to perform: safeguarding the community's animals, helping occasionally in the fields and looking after their younger brothers and sisters. Boys receive formal education at the village school, although most spend only two years there.

In a Kado courtyard, a tangled line of children troops under the raised arms of two girls (centre). As they duck through the human archway, the children

Schooling for girls is looked on as superfluous; at home, they learn the routines of housewifery and a rudimentary knowledge of the Holy Koran.

None of these duties, though, is onerous. The children's day-to-day existence is remarkably carefree, especially during the summer months when there is no school. Youngsters are indulged by their parents and grandparents, and accompany their fathers to markets and fairs. But they have no need to be entertained by adults; the lanes and compounds of the village echo with their noisy enthusiasm as they roam unhindered, playing the games that the world's children have played since time began.

chant in unison, "Have you seen my beloved?" They then go on to act out an ancient rhyme that tells of the legendary marriage of a king's daughter.

Clutching a veil, a girl pursues another round a circle of sitting children. The game starts when one player drops the veil behind a seated child's back. Thus chosen, the sitting child must leap up, snatch the veil and use it to touch the first player before she can reach the empty place in the circle.

Two girls secretly pass a pebble between them while young children huddle on the ground with averted eyes and an amused boy looks on. To play the game, each crouching child must guess who holds the pebble; those who guess rightly are bundled to one spot—"heaven"—while children who make the wrong choice are picked up and thrown into "hell". The losers must offer a forfeit, such as singing a song.

Holding one leg while hopping about on the other, boys try to topple one another to the ground. The aggressive spirit of the game makes it a favourite of Pathan youths, who play it frequently up to the age of 15 or 16.

Counterbalancing each other, two young sisters whirl on ropes round a knotty pole located on bare ground in front of the village school. Despite the

simplicity of the contraption, the children rotating on it can achieve dizzying speed, by which the most daring performers reach a considerable height.

Two | **Honour's Uncompromising Code**

My life in Shams-ud Din's household settled down into a pattern of relaxed conversation, punctuated by prayers five times a day at prescribed hours and by cups of sweet tea that arrived at random intervals throughout the day. The peaceful routine was far removed from what I expected in the wake of the violent tales I had heard about the Pathans and I was coming to enjoy the companionable way in which the Kado villagers passed their time. Usually there were at any given time about half a dozen men relaxing in the *hujra*— the majority of them relatives of Shams-ud Din. In addition, visitors would drop by to pay their respects and provide news more interesting than the commonplaces of Kado itself. From time to time, one or two of the men would leave to attend to some necessary task in the fields, but their places would soon be taken by others, returning for a respite.

Despite the rough environment of the *hujra,* much of what I experienced— the susurrus of talk, the tobacco smoke, above all the exclusively masculine atmosphere—would not have been out of place in a genteel London club. The recurring topics of conversation—the rising cost of living, the price of land, the lack of respect of youth for age—would also have had close parallels. But there the surface similarities ended. The rifles my Pathan friends propped casually against their seats, or toyed with absent-mindedly as they talked, were a constant visual reminder of the exotic ambience. In addition, the scent of tobacco did not come from Havana cigars but from a hubble-bubble: a pipe shaped like a bulbous flower vase, filled with water to cool the acrid smoke of locally grown tobacco.

Even without the sprinkling of hashish favoured by a few of the men, that tobacco can be devastating stuff. On my second day at Kado, in response to an invitation from one of the men, I took a couple of puffs from the bamboo tube that served as the pipe's mouthpiece. I was certain I was going to die: my chest was on fire and my head was awhirl. I had to lie down flat on my back for about a quarter of an hour before I was confident enough to use my feet

again. The villagers who were sitting around me in the *hujra* laughed heartily.

"If you cannot manage a pipe," said one, after I had finally recovered, "you should try taking some *neswar*." And from the loose folds of his clothing he produced a small tin, which he opened to reveal a dark green powder. It was, he told me, just a mixture of ground tobacco and wood ash. He went on to demonstrate its use. He took a healthy pinch between thumb and forefinger, pulled his lower lip forward with his free hand and placed the powder between his lip and his gums. After a few minutes, during which he extolled the virtues of the substance, he adroitly spat out a gobbet of dark green liquid and, smiling benificently, passed his snuffbox to me.

Warily, I followed his example. The Pathans around me waited for my reaction. At first I was conscious only of a burning sensation; and the unaccustomed presence of the stuff in my mouth made speech difficult, causing me also to dribble. Then, after a minute or two, I began to feel so light-headed that it was very difficult to concentrate. I spat out the snuff in an undignified splutter. I was left once again with a feeling of dizzy intoxication, only this time it took half an hour to dissipate. The explanation was not long in coming: the snuff contained opium.

My companions were hugely amused at my discomfiture. "There's only a pinch of opium in it," the snuff's owner told me. "You can see that it doesn't affect us Pathans." But although I sampled *neswar* several times during my stay, my tolerance level never approached that of the village men.

Each evening, some men left the *hujra* to return to their own compounds; others simply yawned, stretched out on their charpoys and prepared to settle down for the night. Usually, among the latter were Shams-ud Din, his two eldest sons, his brother and a cousin or two. They were joined from time to time by friends who had stayed talking until it was so late that they found it easier to remain overnight than to return in the dark to their homes. Visitors to Kado also spent the night there, even if their business in the village had nothing to do with Shams-ud Din. "Our family is the senior lineage in Kado," his son explained. "Outsiders often sleep in our *hujra* to show respect."

A few days and nights in the calm of the *hujra* had almost persuaded me that the Pathans' reputation for fighting was a thing of their past. Then, at the end of my first week in Kado, an incident occurred that changed my mind abruptly; the placid view I was developing of Pathan society vanished forever.

The night was clear; the heat was almost unbearable. Lying on my charpoy I shut out the stars, the fireflies and the mosquitoes by enveloping myself in a sheet, using the Pathan method I had learnt over the previous days. I lay on my back with one end of the sheet tucked under my feet and the other end over my head; by stretching the sheet taut, I could make a kind of tent between my feet and my head, an airspace that at least gave me an illusion of coolness. Around me, most of the other men had adopted similar positions; a few yards away, Shams-ud Din and his brother gossiped quietly. The only other sound was the occasional scuffle of a dog searching in the grass nearby for the debris of our supper. Despite the heat, I began to drift into sleep.

Then the peace of the Kado night was shattered by the sound of a nearby shot. I yanked the sheet from my face and sat up in alarm. My fellow-guests were already on their feet, rifles in hand, and were moving fast, disappearing among the trees in the direction of the noise. Ihsanullah stayed behind, clasping his own rifle firmly. He had no ready explanation for the shot, he said; it might be a raiding party from a rival Mohmand clan or even from Pathans of the Afridi tribe. The men were always on guard for such a thing, he continued, and with good reason: a year rarely went by without at least one villager in Kado being killed or injured, the victim of one continuing dispute or another. I was less than reassured. It was one thing to have a theoretical knowledge of the Pathans' propensity for feuding; it was quite another to be caught up in a practical demonstration of tribal violence. Waiting in the open, I felt uncomfortably like a target in a shooting gallery.

The men returned about a quarter of an hour later, talking animatedly but showing no signs of tension. After a brief discussion with his father, who had accompanied the impromptu guard, Ihsanullah came over to me. There had been no trouble, he said. A distant cousin had just returned to the village from a shopping expedition with several boxes of rifle ammunition he had smuggled in from outside the tribal territory. Impatient to test the bullets, he had fired one into the air as an experiment. No harm had been done; the men around me, settling back into their sleeping positions, were clearly amused by the incident—although they all cursed the perpetrator as a fool.

Still, their instantaneous reaction to the alarm suggested that they had a good deal of experience of everyday violence. I now felt definitely less secure. I tried to relax again but my mummified shape thrashed about far longer than it would have done earlier that evening.

By the time I surfaced, at dawn, the men had already prayed. With breakfast in front of me and comforted by the early morning light, I felt confident enough to ask Ihsanullah to explain why he and his cousins lived in fear of trouble from their neighbours. "Well," he began uncomfortably, "you see,

Perched on a hillside, tribesmen on a
hunting trip keep a sharp look-out for game.
Their likely bag will consist only of rabbits or
wild goats, since their expert marksmanship
has cleared the hunting grounds of the
leopards and the deer that once abounded.

we are in the middle of a kidnapping case right now. And the kidnappers are Afridis." "You mean, someone from Kado has been kidnapped?" I asked, my agitation rising again. "No, no," said Ihsanullah. "It's not a person, it's a car." And he went on to explain the "car-napping".

"In the old days, when caravans passed through and would not pay the tribute due to us, we often kidnapped one of their people and held him until they gave us what we wanted. And while the British were here, when there were still Hindu villages in the plain near Peshawar, we would sometimes kidnap a merchant or one of his family and take him into the mountains until we got a good ransom for him. I even heard of English people being taken. But not by us," he added hastily. "By Afridis or Wazirs. That was all a long time ago, of course. The British left and the Hindus fled to India when Pakistan became independent, and we don't kidnap people any more. At the moment, though, there is a dispute between us Mohmands and some Afridis from Jamrud, at the mouth of the Khyber Pass. No one has been injured yet, but one night the Afridis came and kidnapped a car from Kado."

Car kidnapping, it transpired, had become a regular practice. Tribal Pathans would steal a car from one of the towns in the settled area, drive it back into the mountains and then demand money for its return. Even high-ranking army officers or government officials were not exempt from this form of extortion. And the practice was highly effective: since there was no easy way to track down vehicles hidden among the mountains of the tribal territory, it made more sense for the unfortunate victims to pay the money demanded than to refuse and have their cars disappear forever.

Mohmands themselves own very few cars; even the most battered jalopy is therefore a treasured possession, prized as much for the status it confers as for its utility as transport in the largely roadless tribal territories. It was the car's symbolic value, not its monetary worth, that had interested the Jamrud Afridis. They had a personal feud against one of the Kado villagers, whom they accused of owing money on a land transaction. In fact, the car they stole did not belong to their enemy; it was the property of one of his fellow clansmen. But to the Pathans' way of thinking, that was good enough: the car's hapless owner, the Afridis hoped, would put enough pressure on his kinsman to make him pay the money they considered due to them.

However, the Afridis had underestimated the men of Kado. It would have been shameful to yield meekly to outside pressure, Ihsanullah explained. Instead, his tribal comrades in retaliation had raided Jamrud and kidnapped an Afridi car, which they had hidden in the Kado area. No wonder they were expecting trouble! It seemed to me that the dispute could easily escalate from car stealing to bloodshed; and judging by the expression on Ihsanullah's face, I could see he agreed. But honour was at stake, he told me firmly, and neither side was prepared to discuss compromise.

There was no sign in Kado that day of the conflict that bubbled beneath the peaceful surface of everyday life; and it would have been tactless of me to ask too many direct questions. But as time passed, I began to learn about the hidden preoccupations of the quiet, hospitable men with whom I was living. I

discovered that the car kidnapping case was only one of at least a dozen continuing feuds in which the village menfolk were involved.

As Ihsanullah had indicated, the quarrelsome behaviour of his fellow Pathans was dictated by their concept of honour. "Just because a man is born in a Pathan village and his parents are Pathan," he explained, "that is not enough to make him a Pathan—a true Pukhtun. He must also follow *pukhtunwali*." The code of *pukhtunwali* rules almost every aspect of Pathan life. Broadly speaking, the code decrees what is honourable behaviour for a man and what is not; it requires that hospitality be extended to all strangers and refugees; it demands that the chastity of women be protected; but, above all, it absolutely insists on revenge for injury or insult. The code is simple and it is written only in the hearts of Pathans.

The treatment that Toby and I received during our stay in Kado was determined by *pukhtunwali*. When Shams-ud Din first invited us to his village, he had been following the code; it was the behaviour expected of a Pathan elder. His fellow tribesmen would note that he had done Pukhtu and that he was now responsible for our welfare. Any interference with us would be regarded as an insult to him, and insults would be revenged. For Ihsanullah, as well, it was simple: "If my father did not retaliate when insults were done to him or to those under his protection, even over small matters, then people would not believe that he was a true Pathan."

I had seen that "revenge" could consist of the kidnapping of an old car; that was in a minor affair, where no blood had been spilt. I was soon to discover the lengths to which Pathans would go in more serious matters. One morning, during my third week in Kado, I was resting in the *hujra*, listening to one old tribesman begin his regular harangue on the outrageous cost of land, when our group was disturbed by the arrival of four heavily armed men. I had not seen them before. Although they were greeted politely by the Kado men, they were not invited to stay. They shook hands with everyone and

A nomad tribesman winds a long strip of orange cloth round his head to make a turban. Each Pathan group favours a distinctive style or colour. Turbans are often replaced by simple skull caps, but only young boys or the very poor go bareheaded.

exchanged a few words, then continued along a path towards the mountains.

I was informed that the men were outlaws. Their home was Janat, a Mohmand village just outside the tribal territories. Now they lived with their families on the farthest edge of Kado, close to the mountains that would offer them an escape route in case of attack. Despite their load of weaponry, they had simply been working in the fields; no outlaw dared to spend a moment unarmed. I was consumed with curiosity; but to satisfy it I had to wait until the next day, when Ihsanullah arranged for one of the four men to tell me his story. It swept away any romantic ideas I had ever had of outlawry.

With Ihsanullah, I went to the outlaw's compound. It was similar in design to Shams-ud Din's, but exhibiting unmistakable signs of poverty and general shabbiness. The man offered us tea before he began. "My name is Nur Said," he said. "I lived with my family in Janat, where we owned several fields. We had a hard life in that place. There was barely enough irrigation water in the canals and for years we had to argue with an upstream clan to get our quota. They were always unwilling to allow us a fair share. Then one year they cut off our water altogether. We complained, of course, and made many requests to the authorities and to the elders of the village. But for a whole year nothing was done. We continued to lose our water—and our crops. I talked the business over with my elder brother. Finally, we decided that the only way we would get justice was by taking our water back by force. After all, it was not only a matter of livelihood, it had become a matter of honour."

Nur Said paused long enough to send a boy for more tea before continuing. "My brother and I took our guns and went to the fields to lie in wait for our enemies. But they did not appear, so we blocked their irrigation channels with mud and stones. We knew that they would have to come and dig the channels clear again. When three of their men eventually arrived, it was night. My brother opened fire first, but he missed. Then I fired. Even though it was dark, I hit one of them and killed him. The other two fled. But instead of returning with guns to fight, they went to the police." Nur Said spat out some snuff. Going to the police, he clearly implied, was behaviour beneath the dignity of a true Pathan. "The police took the man's body to Peshawar and wanted to know who had shot him. My brother and I were named, so we decided to leave the settled lands. We came here, to Kado, where we have some relatives. We knew the police could not follow us into tribal territory.

"But after eight months, we yearned for our land. We could not abandon it, so we went back and gave ourselves up to the police. They put us in prison for a year before we came before the government court, but the court understood that necessity had made us act and we won our case. We returned to our land, intending to farm in peace. Our enemies, though, were angry. They attacked us and killed my brother.

"The killers knew I would take revenge for his death, so they fled to the Khyber district in the tribal territory, where they had friends. Because it was too dangerous to follow them there, the men of my family pretended to leave the village, so that our enemies would be enticed into returning. It was a long wait, but after seven months they came back." Nur Said paused, lost in recol-

lection, and I tried to imagine what it had been like for him. This ordinary-looking man would have lain low in his own village for all those months, never venturing into the fields, where his presence might have been noted and his enemies warned. All the while, he had remained within his family compound, nursing his grievance with an infinite, murderous patience.

"There were three men with me in hiding," Nur Said went on. "My younger brother and two cousins—you met them yesterday. When we heard that our enemies had returned to the village, we prepared an ambush for them, and the next afternoon they fell into our trap. We killed two of them, and wounded another two. Thus Pukhtu was done.

"After that, we had to leave, and quickly. We came back to Kado and we have lived here ever since—even though our enemies say that they are try-ing to arrange terms for peace between us. My mother's brother and my sis-ter's husband have been looking after the land for us. Our enemies dare not attack them; if they did, their families too would join in the quarrel."

Nur Said's case, I came to know, was far from unique. There were many out-laws living in and around Kado. Most were from the settled lands, where the police force as well as avenging kinsmen sought to bring them to book. With the agreement of the Kado villagers, some had gradually managed to acquire land and were slowly integrating into the local society. Others, including Nur Said, worked as labourers or farmed for their hosts in return for the hos-pitality they had been given. In addition to a house, or at least a shelter within a kinsman's compound, that hospitality included a strong element of protec-

Two Kado men engage in an impromptu wrestling match. Pathans indulge in few organized sports, but spontaneous bouts such as this one provide good-humoured and peaceable outlets for high spirits.

tion: as adherents of *pukhtunwali,* the Kado villagers would be expected to take up their own weapons in defence of their guests.

Even cosmopolitan Pathans abide by the tribal code. A few weeks after I talked with the outlaw Nur Said, Shams-ud Din introduced me to a moustached acquaintance whom he respectfully addressed as "doctor". I found it hard to believe that a small tribal village like Kado could boast a doctor of its own but, when I eventually expressed polite scepticism, I was immediately invited to visit the doctor at his home.

Inside his mud-brick shelter, situated on the outskirts of Kado near the Kabul river, was confirmation—a room stacked high with modern medicines that ranged from aspirin to antibiotics. When I asked the doctor what he was doing in such an isolated village, he shrugged philosophically. "I am an outlaw," he said. "If I lived outside the tribal lands, I would be arrested and sent to prison, or attacked by my enemies." Like Nur Said, the doctor had been involved in a dispute concerning land at his home village near Peshawar. A death resulted and five years before he had been obliged to flee. He settled in Kado where, in return for the protection the villagers offered, he dispensed medicine and advice. "I stay here," he told me, "because nowhere else have I received the hospitality my kinsmen have given me." He smiled. "Besides, anywhere else I might be killed."

As we left, the doctor told me how he hoped that in a few years people in his home village would have forgotten all about the dispute that led to his exile. He looked forward to the time when he could move to a major city, such as Karachi or Rawalpindi, and develop his career there. Shams-ud Din said nothing at the time; once we were out of earshot, though, the elder expressed doubt that the doctor would ever be able to leave. "If a feud involves death and honour, it can last forever," he explained. "It would be shameful for the dead man's kin to forget the incident and forgive without taking revenge. If need be, they would follow him to the ends of the earth."

Unresolved disputes are inherited by sons from their fathers. A Pathan proverb expresses the principle succinctly: "A Pathan took his revenge after a hundred years and then said, 'I took it quickly'." In that context, the logic of the code of honour to me seemed inescapable: it appeared possible that every Pathan could be doomed to a violent end in the course of one conflict or another. I said as much to Shams-ud Din.

"To follow the code is not easy," he said. "There are many stories and songs telling of the sorrows of those who do what the code demands. Still, for us it is more important to live as true Pathans than it is to enjoy peace. But there are ways of making peace, too.

"There is the *jirga,* a meeting of the tribal elders that can settle disputes. It may be that you will see a *jirga* in council during your stay. Or marriages can sometimes be arranged to heal the rifts between families. And when there have been too many killings, a man may forgive a murder without shame, provided he does not do so from weakness."

I was sure that Shams-ud Din was thinking of his own experience. I already knew that one bitter, long-term feud had involved members of his own fam-

A village elder (above) daubs his beard with a reddish-orange dye made from finely crushed henna leaves mixed with water. Pathans believe henna not only improves a man's appearance but also wards off the evil eye. While his beard dries, protected by a rag, the tribesman occupies himself by cleaning his cherished rifle (right).

ily, although he himself had not taken an active part. The quarrel was rooted in a part of the code of honour that I found difficult to understand. In the case of Nur Said and the doctor, blood kin had banded together against outsiders. But there is another aspect of *pukhtunwali*—perhaps the most ferocious of all—that sets cousin against cousin and can lead to years of internecine warfare. Pathans call this kind of affair *tarboorwali* and it derives from the word *tarboor*, meaning "father's brother's son". Traditionally, Pathan cousins who are related through the male line strive with one another for dominance within their clan and lineage. Inevitably, hatred grows out of such constant rivalry and when conflicts do occur they are likely to take a deadly form. An old Pathan proverb offers ruthless advice: "When he is little, play with him; when he is grown up, he is a cousin: kill him." Pathans being Pathans, the killing is unlikely to stop there.

The murderous custom of *tarboorwali* explains much of Pathan history. It is the main reason why so few great leaders come to power among them, why the tribes remain so fragmented politically, and why their egalitarian way of life has persisted through the centuries. No man can rise far above others when his own cousins are guaranteed to be his most implacable enemies. As a system of checks and balances ensuring the continuation of traditional tribal life, *tarboorwali* has been highly effective. But its cost in blood has been appalling, as the feud that had shaken Shams-ud Din's family showed.

The affair began in the 1930s, when Shams-ud Din's mother's brother was shot dead by his own cousin. Ostensibly, the reason for the killing was competition between the two men over a marriageable widow. In fact, cousin rivalry itself was the cause of the dispute: the two men would have confronted each other sooner or later regardless of the widow. But, once the first blood had been shed, the quarrel acquired a momentum of its own, as aggrieved kinsmen looked for revenge to satisfy their own honour and sought out allies who would extend the fighting. The feud lasted for more than 20 years and, by the time it was over, eight men had died—a heavy loss for a small interrelated community to bear. Shams-ud Din had lost several uncles; the widening ripples of the quarrel had drawn in his wife's family, too, and the father and brother of his wife, Bebeha, were also among the dead.

In the end, the exhaustion of passion made it possible for the participants to arrange peace; and memories of the damage inflicted in homage to honour helped to keep that peace. Also, the increasing prosperity of Kado had undoubtedly encouraged co-operation among close relatives. That was something I would learn more about as the weeks passed. But I had seen enough to appreciate that the potential for violence was always there, ready to be called into reality at a moment's notice.

After I had been in Kado about a month, Shams-ud Din invited me to join a party of villagers on a journey to the source of most of the local weaponry: the town of Darra Adam Khel, about 40 miles from Kado, in Afridi tribal territory to the south of Peshawar. I knew there was little love lost between at least some Afridis and my Mohmand hosts, but Shams-ud Din assured me that the trip would be safe. In the first place, we would travel on the main roads, where the rule of the Pakistan Government was both established and respected. We would follow the road out of the tribal area at Michni, journey through the settled lands and re-enter tribal territory close to Darra. In any case, he explained, Darra was too important an arms source for fighting to be tolerated in its precincts; Pathans from all over Pakistan and even from across the border in Afghanistan went there for their guns and ammunition. It was from Darra that the Kado villager had returned with the bullets he had inconsiderately tested in the middle of the night. And almost every weapon in Kado—other than a few cherished trophies from the days of battle with the British—was made there.

Darra was an extraordinary place. Its main street was crowded with tur-banned men. Buffaloes and cattle weaved among the cars and trucks. Armed Pathans strolled casually in groups from one doorway to another. Garish hand-lettered signs emblazoned on the hundred or so shop fronts pro-claimed the weapons their proprietors had for sale. From the alley-ways between the doorways came the clangour of gunsmiths hard at work. The "London Arms Store" specialized in replica British rifles; Abdel Kharim's la-vishly painted shop front proudly boasted that his business was established in 1880. A little further along the Brothers Said were selling guns disguised as umbrellas and fountain pens—and happily advertised their wares by firing them into the air outside their shop.

Shams-ud Din had come to Darra to replace his worn-out rifle, itself a Darra product. Accompanied by his cheerful travelling companions, we went from shop to shop, inspecting, haggling and joking; it was obvious that everyone

Elders relax over a board game in which stones and seeds are used as counters on an improvised grid that is scratched on the hard ground. Between the players stands a hubble-bubble, a giant pipe containing water to filter fumes from the strong tobacco that Pathans occasionally lace with hashish.

derived as much pleasure from the bargaining process—and the exchange of gossip—as they did from the beautifully made bolt-action rifle that Shams-ud Din finally decided to purchase.

It was decided we should return by the route we had come by: via the settled area. Even had the Mohmands been on good terms with the Afridis, going back to Kado through tribal territory would have meant a longer and more arduous journey over poor or non-existent roads. However, Shams-ud Din's new rifle threatened to complicate matters: the Pakistan Government understandably disapproved of armed Pathans wandering in the settled area. The weapon would have to be smuggled through.

Shams-ud Din chose to take advantage of the delivery service offered through the shopkeepers by Darra's professional smugglers. Such men have contacts at the border posts, he explained, and it was worth the small extra cost to ensure that his rifle would arrive safely in Kado. It never occurred to him that he might be cheated of his purchase; the unknown smuggler would be a Pathan, too, and accepting responsibility for delivery involved his personal honour. The rifle turned up at Kado two days after our return.

For Shams-ud Din there was no question that his purchase had been worth all the trouble, as well as the considerable amount of money spent on it. But although the handsome acquisition had great importance as a symbol, its practical value would clearly be very limited: I found that Mohmands not actively involved in blood feuds had very little to shoot at. Long ago, the tribesmen had rejoiced in hunting wildcats, leopards, and various species of deer and goat in the mountains behind Kado. But their very expertise so depleted the game that opportunities to pursue the pastime had become few.

However, one hunting expedition did take place during my stay. Three relatives of Shams-ud Din decided that their fields were in good enough shape to go untended for a few days and we set off together for the Mohmand Hills behind Kado. Hunting, they assured me, was one of the best ways to practise marksmanship, as well as being the most challenging of sports.

We left at dawn, on what was to be a three-day trip. I was going to accompany them only for the first ten miles or so: I knew that once we got into rough country, I would only slow the hunters down. They wore their everyday clothes and, in the circumstances, I was surprised at how colourful they were: combinations of blue, yellow, brown and green. It seemed odd that a people so renowned for mountain fighting and the tactics of the ambush should choose to be so conspicuous. But once we had reached the mountain country I changed my mind. Here, the landscape itself was multicoloured, although its shades of yellow, brown and blue-grey were not obvious in the wash of sunlight. But the light had the same effect on the clothing of the three Pathans, so that they merged effortlessly into their surroundings; when they halted, it was difficult to detect them against the background, even when they sat together in one spot.

After a few hours, I wished them luck and turned back. They strode off at an easy pace carrying their blankets, some dried milk, bread and their weapons. I stopped now and then to watch them, occasionally silhouetted on a ridge-

A villager indulges in a snuff made from ground tobacco leaves mixed with wood ash and a little opium. Just a pinch of the mixture is inserted behind the lower lip. Snuff-taking, widespread among males, has the usual side effects including tooth decay and a compulsion to spit; young men who hold out against its use are considered by their conservative elders to be worthy of praise.

line, more often blending into the rocky hillsides. Eventually, they vanished over a nearby peak. I retraced my steps to Kado to await their return.

As everyone had expected, the results of the hunting trip were paltry. In three days, they shot only three rabbits and, since no one in Kado liked rabbit meat, the expedition had to be written off as pure sport. Their lack of success was not due to want of effort; the three hunters had climbed the highest peaks in the area—about 4,000 feet—but even from such vantage points they had not seen any game worth following. At these high altitudes, night temperatures fell close to freezing and the three men had slept wrapped tightly in their blankets in the shelter of a rock or in a cave mouth huddled round a fire. It seemed to me that it had been an uncomfortable sort of pastime, but the three men appeared satisfied enough.

Obviously, what constitutes amusement varies with the culture. Aside from hunting, the men of Kado had few forms of entertainment. Occasionally, two youths would indulge in a spontaneous wrestling match, to the accompaniment of loud cheers and jeers from their fellows, and on feast days everyone enjoyed a cockfight. A really special occasion might be marked by something much more exciting—a fight to the death between two full-grown bull buffaloes. The local buffaloes were ill-tempered creatures, and only a little goading was necessary to provoke them into mutual aggression. But such contests were few and far between, for the animals were far too valuable as beasts of burden to be sacrificed for a few hours' sport.

Every amusement, it seemed, involved—in greater or lesser degree—a form of violence. So it came as some surprise when I saw Shams-ud Din's brother sitting quietly on the ground with a friend and enjoying a peaceful game of *manzareh*: moving black seeds and white stones on a pattern of squares marked in the dusty earth. After only a few minutes, however, the game degenerated into a fierce argument, as the two grey-bearded men angrily disputed each other's moves. Soon, though, the players were cackling with laughter. Nevertheless, the image of the two elders, engaged in a game governed by complex rules and likely to erupt at any moment into violence, encapsulated what I had learnt about the Pathan psyche—so far.

Hand-Made Counterfeit Weapons

The small town of Darra Adam Khel, located in the tribal territories near
Peshawar, has a unique stock-in-trade. Crowded into the dusty half mile of
its only street are more than a hundred gunshops that offer Pathans
ingenious copies of the world's best-known rifles, pistols and machine-
guns. Replicas of British Lee-Enfields are displayed beside those of
Russian Kalashnikovs and U.S. Colts. Hammered out of scrap steel by
Darra's industrious gunsmiths, each weapon carries a convincing serial
number and company trademark to impress prospective buyers. Pathan
craftsmen have been plying their trade in the town for at least 200 years,

Cooled by a large electric fan, an elderly Pathan craftsman uses a hammer and chisel to form a pistol magazine from a piece of scrap sheet metal. The

using only hand-tools and a few primitive lathes to produce a wide range of lethal armaments. Although poor materials make the counterfeit weapons less reliable than the assembly line originals, demand among Pathans exceeds supply and customers will pay as much as a year's cash income for a well-turned rifle. At such a price, a tribesman will spend days haggling and comparing before he parts with the money for what may be a once-in-a-lifetime purchase. Afterwards, he may face a further expense: the hiring of a professional smuggler to sneak his acquisition through frontier checkpoints between Darra and his own tribal enclave.

wooden boxes ranged along the wall behind him contain a selection of low-grade steel rods, the raw material used in the manufacture of rifle barrels.

A gunsmith uses pincers to hold a glowing
steel rod against a low anvil, while his burly
colleague swings a hammer to form the
metal—rendered malleable by a spell in a
mud furnace (centre)—into a breechblock.

The glowing frame of an automatic pistol is
left to cool before being filed into final
shape. It will take one man a full week to
make the other parts and assemble the
whole weapon, a copy of a Spanish Astra.

A workman uses a traditional bow-drill to bore neat screw-holes in a set of pistol handgrips. The bowstring is looped round the drill shaft; as the bow is moved from side to side, the shaft is made to rotate.

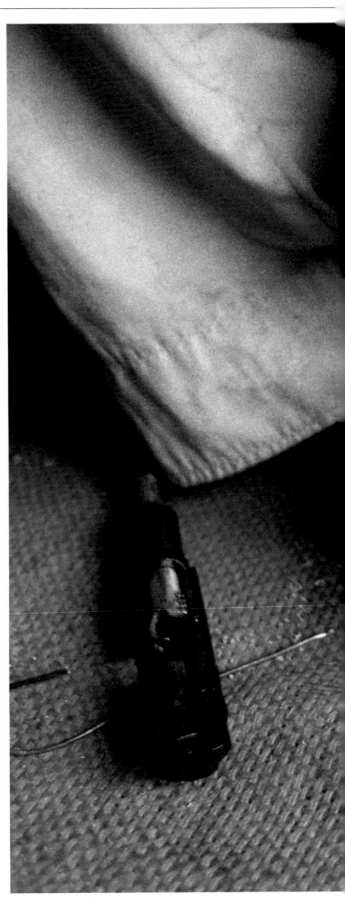

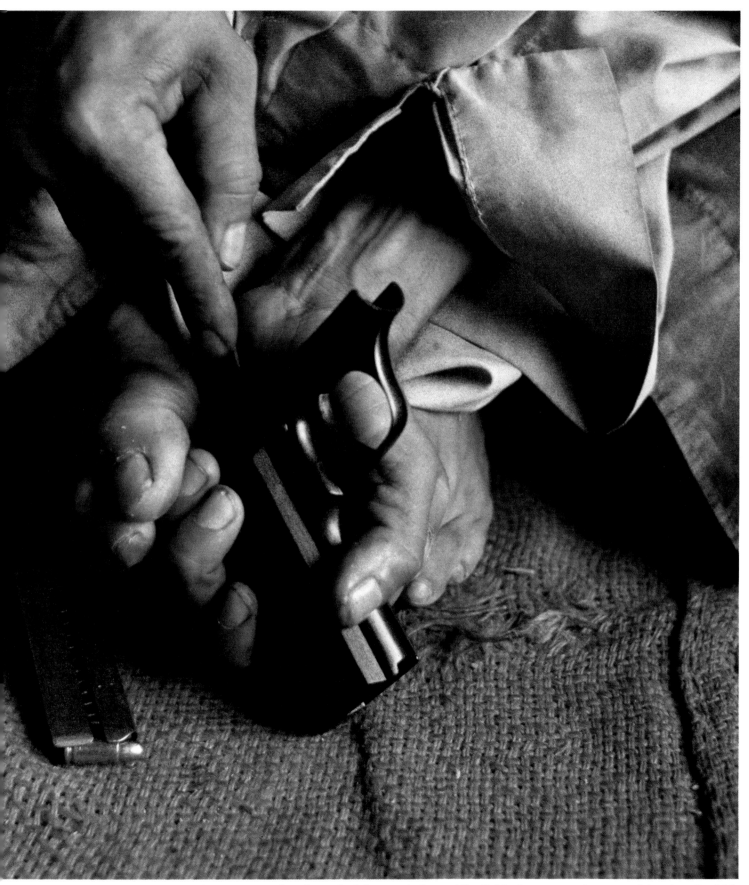

Making adroit use of both fingers and toes, a gunsmith performs the delicate task of assembling finished components into a complete automatic pistol.

Such is the dexterity of Darra's weapon counterfeiters that only trained eyes can detect the difference between the genuine Astra Falcon pistol and its replica. The dark handgrip of the original (top) has been secured by screws whose slots are perfectly centred; those in the copy are off-centre.

Fake trademarks, ordnance stamps and serial numbers add convincing touches to these counterfeit small arms, copied mostly from British originals. The markings are meaningless to the gunsmiths who duplicate them, but help to inspire trust in the buyer. One wildly inaccurate example (bottom row, right) juxtaposes a modern date with the insignia of British Imperial rule.

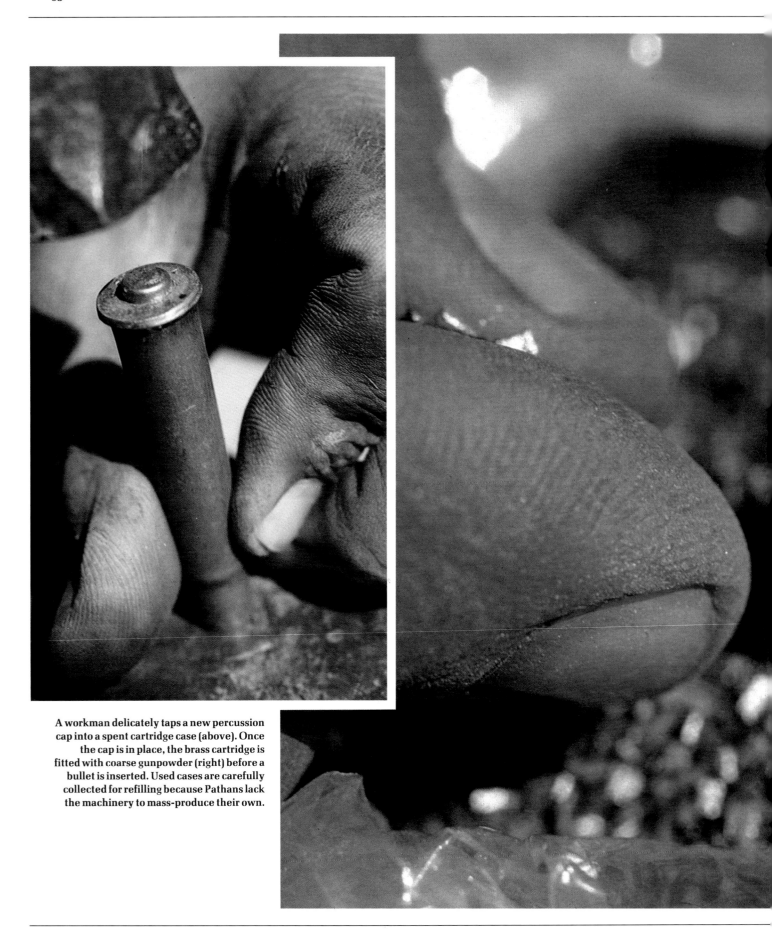

A workman delicately taps a new percussion cap into a spent cartridge case (above). Once the cap is in place, the brass cartridge is fitted with coarse gunpowder (right) before a bullet is inserted. Used cases are carefully collected for refilling because Pathans lack the machinery to mass-produce their own.

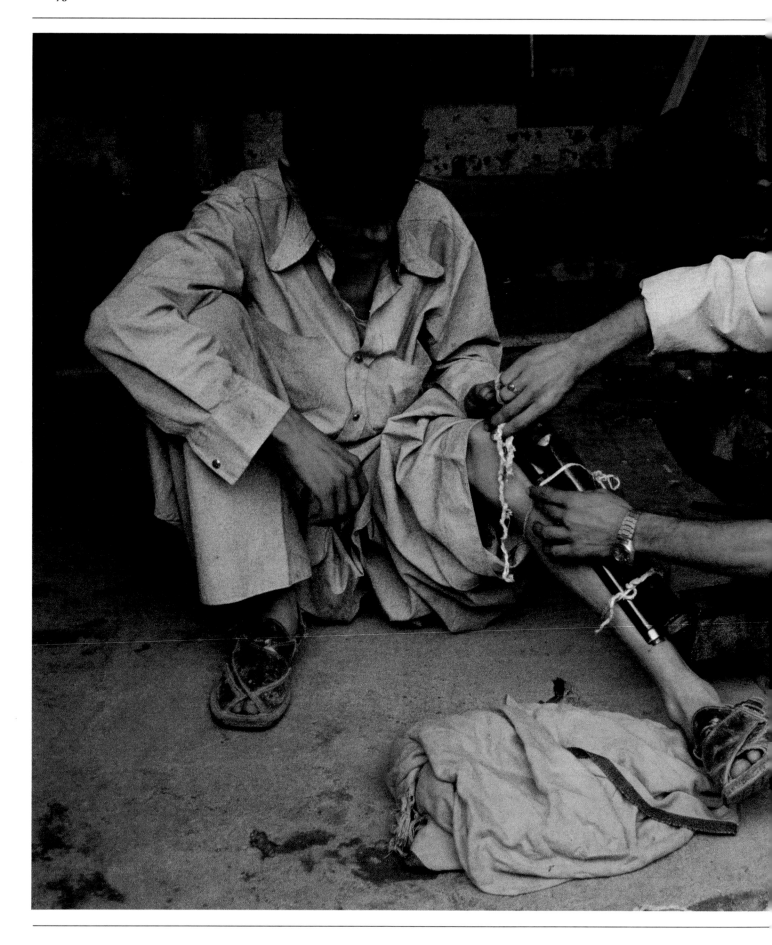

A smuggler watches while sections of a newly bought Lee-Enfield rifle—a favourite Pathan weapon since the days of the British Raj—are tied to his leg. Other parts will be strapped elsewhere on his body, hidden beneath the folds of his loose clothing.

Three | A Special Destiny for Women

I had known in advance that the Mohmand women would keep their distance from me, but I had not realized how complete would be their seclusion. While the men chatted amicably in their *hujra* and children of both sexes played their laughing games around the village, the women spent most of their time in the shelter of the walled courtyards. If a woman left the security of the compound to work in the open fields or to wash clothes in an irrigation canal, I was always led by a discreetly circuitous route that kept her out of my sight. The overall effect was a little unnerving: Kado, it seemed, was populated only by men and children.

As the days passed and the villagers began to accept me as a more or less permanent fixture, I did catch sight of some women, walking or occasionally working near their family compounds. But the only faces I saw belonged to girls younger than 12, playing in the village with their brothers, or grandmothers, who seemed to be at least 60, going from doorway to doorway on some inscrutable business of their own. Any woman between these ages was well covered, either by a *burqa*, an ankle-length garment that enshrouded her completely, with only a strip of mesh at eye level through which she could see; or by a *chaddar*, a cloth draped over the head that could be pulled instantly across the face, concealing every feature but the eyes. A standard procedure governed every encounter. When a woman saw me, even at a distance, she would turn her back at once and, if she was wearing a *chaddar*, quickly cover her face. For my part, as instructed, I would cast my eyes groundwards and pass by hurriedly without looking in the direction of the veiled figures. This concealment is the meaning of purdah.

The word itself is a Persian term for a curtain, which originally gave privacy to the women's quarters of households wealthy enough to afford them. It has come to mean the whole system of restraints under which many Muslim women must live. Purdah has been observed in some form or another in most Islamic societies, but it was not a part of the early Muslim way of life. It originated in the 10th or 11th century, 300 years or more after the death of the

Prophet Muhammad. Although the Koran does not clearly demand purdah, Islamic scholars were able to justify it by citing Koranic texts: "Tell the believing women to lower their gaze, and be modest, and not to display their adornment except that which is apparent, and to draw their veils over their bosoms, and not to reveal their adornment save to their husbands, fathers or their sons, or their own women, or their slaves, or male attendants who lack vigour, or children who know naught of women's nakedness."

On the subject of the veil, the Koran enjoins: "O Prophet! Tell thy wives and thy daughters and the women of the believers to draw cloaks close around themselves. That will be better, so they may be recognized and not teased . . . As for women past child-bearing age, who have no hope of marriage, it is no sin for them if they discard their clothing in such a way as not to show adornment, but to refrain is better for them."

The texts are interpreted differently all over the Muslim world, but few people adopt a more rigid observance than do the Pathans. The women whom I glimpsed spent most of their lives behind Kado's high walls, out of sight of strangers. When a woman worked in the fields, she kept her veil on her head and bared her face only when she was certain she was unobserved.

Still, the effects of purdah are easier for women to endure in a tribal village than they would be in a large town. For a woman may walk freely—although always discreetly—in the presence of her male relatives; it is only from strangers that she must conceal herself. Among Mohmand Pathans, most marriages are contracted to relations, usually living in the same area, and the kinship of blood and marriage that united the people of Kado extended the circle of a woman's freedom from a single compound to most of the village.

In a town or city, however, where kinsmen would be few and strangers many, it seemed to me that a woman's life would be unbearable. Even in Kado the pressures were considerable. The machinery of purdah—the high walls, the separation of the sexes, the constraints on a woman's ability to work or even to attend to such mundane pursuits as shopping—greatly com-

Seated at a shoe stall in a Peshawar bazaar, a Pathan chooses a pair of leather sandals for his wife. Because custom prevents a woman from entering such a public place as a market, the wife gives her husband a piece of string cut to the length of her foot.

which was reserved for the women. I suppose they went outside the compound into the fields or along the river."

As the barriers of reserve lowered, Bebeha and her daughters-in-law showed themselves endlessly curious about the outside world—and about how Toby herself lived. What they found hardest to understand was how Toby, a married woman, could find herself in the company of another man and away from her husband. The Kado women could just about grasp that other societies did not observe the rules of purdah, although from their orthodox Islamic viewpoint such behaviour was almost incomprehensible— and certainly regrettable. But surely, they asked Toby, her situation was one that must bring dishonour on the family?

"I had to spend hours showing them photos of my husband and children," Toby later told me, "and explaining that I was in Kado with my husband's agreement. They kept asking about you. I said that you were like a brother, that we worked together and that my husband expected you to protect his honour by looking after me. But they found this hard to accept. After all, they had to be wary even about being seen by a strange man."

Toby's relief at her acceptance into the household was soon overshadowed by a new worry. How could she persuade the women of the village to be photographed? This required the permission of their husbands, and even after that was given they were still reluctant. An attempt at a simple picture—a woman with her back to the camera, making bread—often ended with the woman fleeing from the courtyard until Toby had put the camera away. The problem was overcome by Bebeha. With the full support of Shams-ud Din

On their way to visit a holy man's tomb, two women escorted by an older male relative are slowly ferried across the wide Kabul river. To propel the boat, a boy hauls on a rope stretched tautly from bank to bank, while another heaves on an oar to hold the boat at right angles to the river's current.

and his sons, she and her daughters-in-law allowed Toby to photograph them wherever and whenever she wanted. Their example—and Bebeha's coaxing—were effective in persuading other women to confront the camera.

Over the weeks, Toby developed a warm relationship with Bebeha, and through her gained unique insight into the pleasures and problems of Pathan women. "Bebeha must have been very beautiful," said Toby. "But now she looks old for her age—she can hardly be older than her mid-forties. She works so hard. She seems to see to everything."

As befitted her status, Bebeha received many visits from female friends and relatives, mostly from Kado but occasionally from villages further afield, seeking advice, wishing to discuss village issues such as forthcoming marriages or simply being sociable. In turn, she would call on other women in the village. When she left her courtyard, she was always veiled; but the *burqa* was reserved for rare trips outside the village. During our stay, she left the village on only two occasions—once to go to a wedding in the village of Bela, just outside the tribal lands, and once to visit the tomb of a holy man, where she prayed for her grandsons' health. She never went to market, even in the nearby town of Shabkadar; all her shopping, from her clothes to the few items of food not supplied by the family fields, was done by Shams-ud Din.

But despite all the restrictions on her daily life, Bebeha seemed to be a contented woman. "There was a strong feeling of mutual affection and respect between Shams-ud Din and Bebeha," Toby recalled. "When I went outside the courtyard with Shams-ud Din alone, he would always insist on carrying my heavy camera bag—because I was a guest, not because I was a woman. But if Bebeha was with us, she would have to carry it; Shams-ud Din could not allow himself to be seen carrying something for his wife. When Bebeha and I carried the bag together, he smiled and looked away.

"When the two of them settled down together by the small courtyard fire to have tea and a discussion of the day's events, it seemed to be very much a conversation between equals. Pathans are not given to public endearment between man and wife. But once, I remember Shams-ud Din repeating the words of a song we had just heard some women singing. It was a sentimental song. Each verse ended with the refrain 'My beloved'. When the song was over, Shams-ud Din put his arms round Bebeha and, laughing, pointed at her as he repeated the last line, 'My beloved'."

A Day in the Life of **Bebeha**

As day broke over the mountain peaks, the grey morning dusk began to thin inside the walls of the courtyard, where a row of charpoys held the sleeping forms of several women and children. Just outside the walls, the men of the family lay on similar charpoys.

Within the compound, one of the women flung back the cotton quilt that had protected her from the freshness of the night, while the others lay muffled and unmoving. Bebeha, wife of Shams-ud Din, usually got up first—just as she went to bed last. A vigorous and good-natured woman in her mid-forties, Bebeha reigned as the undisputed mistress of the household. The four eldest of her seven children were already married; the two grown-up sons slept outside in the *hujra* and the two married daughters had joined their husbands' households. Bebeha's three youngest children—two boys and a girl—lay sleeping within the compound.

Wearing the light veil, tunic and loose trousers she had slept in, Bebeha fetched a few sticks from the woodpile and started a fire. While the wood was catching, she first washed her face, hands and feet briefly with a little water from an earthenware jar, and said the first of Islam's five daily prayers, kneeling on the porch where she had spread a mat. Soon the sound of the crackling fire carried through the still morning air.

Her two daughters-in-law stirred and Bebeha called to them to help her. The elder—the wife of Ihsanullah, her first son—lowered a bucket into the well at one side of the yard and drew up water. She filled a kettle with water and set it on the fire that Bebeha had started. The house was one of the few in the village to have its own well, which provided, at a depth of 12 to 15 feet, a limited quantity of clean, clear water for drinking and cooking; for other purposes, the family fetched water from a tributary of the Kabul river five minutes' walk away, just as the rest of the villagers did. The other daughter-in-law, the wife of Bebeha's second son Farmanullah, fetched

Women and children breakfast on tea and bread.

Children help catch a chicken for lunch.

dishes from a closed cupboard set in a wall by the cooking area, and from a storage basket she produced small flat loaves of bread made the day before.

Meanwhile, Bebeha milked the two buffaloes—one of them with a calf—that were tethered under a lean-to shelter. She added milk, tea and sugar to the kettle and let them boil together for a few minutes. By the time the tea was ready, Bebeha's younger children—Ghani Rahman, 14, Haji Rahman, 8, and their sister Roquia, 11—were awake. Three little grandchildren slumbered on.

About 6 a.m., Bebeha carried a pile of bread and the tea kettle to the men where they had slept, and returned to find the women and children sitting together drinking tea and eating bread on to which a little ghee—clarified butter—had been poured.

The courtyard was the women's province, but the men of the family entered and left without formalities. This morning, Ihsanullah and Shams-ud Din, who were planning a visit to the city of Peshawar 15 miles away, came in along with Farmanullah to change their clothes for the trip and to consult the women about the purchases they were to make in the Peshawar bazaar. Often, one of the young boys would accompany the men simply for the outing, but this time the men were going alone.

Once Shams-ud Din and Ihsanullah had left, Farman (as he was known in the family) lingered for a while playing with his little nephew, two-year-old Ekranullah, and

his own baby boy Redwanullah, who had just had his first birthday. Farman's day would be spent as usual, mostly in the fields, since he had been given overall responsibility for managing all the family's land. At this time—the end of April—the wheat was ripe and he was busy every day harvesting the fields.

But before Farman left, Bebeha had a job for him. As a special treat, she had decided to have a chicken for lunch, and the younger children, Roquia and Haji Rahman, had helped her corner one of the athletic birds that were pecking and scratching around the yard. Bebeha asked Farman to kill it for her; in Islam only a man may kill an animal and only a woman may gut it. Farman used a stone to sharpen his knife and took the bird outside the compound, where he slit its throat and allowed the blood to run into the dust. Then he cut off the bird's head and feet, handed the carcass back to Bebeha and left for his morning's work.

With Roquia watching and helping her, Bebeha plucked, cleaned and cut up the newly killed chicken, and put the pieces—along with onion, spices and a little water—in a light aluminium pan that she had made sturdy and heat-retaining with a jacket of hardened clay. Adding more fuel to the cooking fire in the little open hearth on the porch, she set the pot on it to simmer, so that the chicken would be ready for lunch at about 11.30. Then Bebeha and her daughters-in-law set about

Daily chores begin with tidying the courtyard.

Kneading dough for bread is a twice-daily task.

their household chores. First they set the courtyard in order for the day. The cotton-fibre-filled quilts from the charpoys were slung on the clothes line to air, and two charpoys were picked up from the centre of the yard and set back against the walls, to leave the space free for the comings and goings of the day. The quilt covers had been made at home from printed cloth bought in the Peshawar bazaar, as had the women's own clothes.

When the women had finished tidying the compound, Ihsanullah's wife asked her sister-in-law to help move the heavy wooden cradle in which her month-old baby napped during the day. They put it in the shade of the tree, where anyone—child or adult—who happened to be near could keep an eye on the baby and perhaps swing the cradle from time to time in passing.

Bebeha next turned to sifting flour into a broad shallow bowl, to make fresh bread for the next meal. She mixed a little water with the flour to form dough, adding a small piece of yesterday's dough to start it rising. After kneading it thoroughly in the bowl, she covered it with a cloth and left it to prove in the shade.

The women did not usually work out of doors, but since Farman was busy with the harvest and the other men of the household had gone to Peshawar, Bebeha now made ready to go out to the barley field that the family cultivated to provide feed for their livestock. The barley was not yet ripe but it was due for weeding and, as an older woman, Bebeha could work in the open field with less risk than her daughters-in-law of offending against the requirements of purdah.

Leaving Ihsanullah's wife to care for her baby and Farman's wife busy repairing a worn quilt, Bebeha called to Roquia. Together they set off at about 10 o'clock for the nearby field. She did not draw her veil over her face even though she was now outside; she knew it was unlikely they would encounter anyone other than female neighbours, all of whom were related to her. And so it turned out: the only people they saw were a group of playful small children who ran past them, bright as a flock of parakeets in their cotton clothes.

At the barley field, no one else was in sight. Bebeha set to work pulling up the sturdy weeds that were growing among the barley stalks. Roquia collected the weeds in a heap at the edge of the field to take back as fresh fodder for the buffaloes. At one moment Bebeha caught sight of the husband of one of her neighbours approaching in the distance. Without stopping her work she drew her shawl over her face and, as soon as the man noticed her, he turned aside and took a different path between the fields, heading for his own crops. As his figure receded Bebeha threw the shawl back again.

From behind the mountains, a thunderous-looking cloud blew up, obscuring the sun but scarcely reducing the oppressive heat. Shortly before 11 o'clock, Bebeha summoned Roquia to her side. The girl gathered up the heap of succulent weeds in her arms and returned with Bebeha to the house.

Bebeha at once set to work preparing lunch. She rapidly formed the now-risen dough into flat oval loaves, pinching off a ball of dough and slapping it from hand to hand with the deftness of a lifetime's experience; the dough almost seemed to shape itself into loaves. She allowed a whole loaf for each adult and a half for each child, with a couple of extra ones to be on the safe side. In all, she put 10 loaves into the bread oven, which was built of clay in

A stint in the barley field occupies part of the morning.

a corner angle of the wall; the bread would be baked and ready to eat in 20 minutes or so.

As she worked—helped as usual by Roquia—Bebeha talked to Ihsanullah's wife, who had just paid a visit to the compound of her own parents and was relaying the family news. Her father was Shams-ud Din's brother, Habibur Rahman, so she and her husband Ihsanullah were first cousins—a spousal relationship preferred by Mohmand Pathans. Actually, the two families were related several times over, because one of Bebeha's elder daughters—considered the beauty of the family—was married to a son of Habibur Rahman. The marriages had taken place at the same time, so that each father had simultaneously given a daughter to his brother's son—the sort of exchange the Pathans find especially satisfactory, since it helps to counteract the rivalry that can flare up between male first cousins, and cancels out the brideprice normally payable by a bridegroom's family to the father of the bride.

A close sympathy had grown up between Bebeha and her first daughter-in-law, a lively, open-minded girl. Much to the family's anxiety, the first four years of her marriage to Ihsanullah had been childless, and the two women had in that interval spent most of their time together. Ihsanullah's first child (luckily a boy) was born about the time Farman married—two years before. Farman's marriage was not an exchange, so his bride had received various presents paid for out of the brideprice, and her wedding decorations of gold and silver paper still hung on the walls of the room within the compound that belonged to the couple. Bebeha sometimes felt sad for Ihsanullah's wife because, unlike her sister-in-law, she owned no sentimental trinkets.

The younger boys had now returned to the compound for lunch; the village school was closed for the summer and the boys were spending most of their time playing around the village and helping the men in the fields. Polio in childhood had left the older boy, 14-year-old Ghani, with a limp that put him at a disadvantage in the hard physical world of the villagers. Ghani was already betrothed to a cousin of his own age, who also had a disability: she was deaf and therefore spoke with difficulty. But she was a girl of considerable intelligence and beauty, and both partners seemed quite content with the

The family gathers for lunch in the courtyard.

A roof-top provides a vantage point . . .   . . . from which Bebeha confers with her next-door neighbour.

match. In two or three years' time, theirs would be another exchange wedding, for Roquia was to marry the brother of the deaf girl.

Under the mulberry tree, the women set the table and spread on it plates of vegetables—tomatoes, potatoes, spinach, sliced onions—the cooked chicken and the newly baked bread. It was an unusually lavish lunch, since summer vegetables were plentiful.

The meal was a cheerful and voluble occasion, informal because Farman was the only grown man then at home. When all the men of the family were present, they usually ate in the women's courtyard; they would be served first, and the women and children would eat after the men had finished. But if the men had male guests, they would take their meal in the *hujra* and one of the younger men of the family would bring the food out to them. On this occasion, Farman's wife served him his food first, but the other women sat down with him and the children lined up in a row on the other side of the table to eat at the same time. When Farman had finished eating, he stayed for a while playing with the children and joining in the conversation. Finally, he left the courtyard to smoke a pipe by the river and then take a nap,

until the midday heat lessened and he could put in more work in the wheat fields. The women never stopped working, moving constantly from one task to another.

When all the children had finished eating, the girls cleared the table and Bebeha, aided by Ihsanullah's wife, washed all the plates, cups and dishes, using sand to scour the cooking pot, then sluicing everything thoroughly with water and setting the utensils out to dry on one of the charpoys.

Leaving her daughter-in-law to put away the dishes and to renew the clay coating on the pot, Bebeha carried a ladder over to one of the rooms built against the outer walls of the compound. She climbed up to the room's flat roof, where some of the newly cut wheat was drying and a few earthenware jars were stored. From there—after making sure there were no strangers next door—she could look straight down into the compound of her neighbour: a close relative and intimate friend, who often came round to bake a couple of loaves in Bebeha's oven, to lend or borrow things, or to fetch some water from her well. On this occasion Bebeha wanted her to grind a little grain for the next day; the villagers sent most of their grain to the mill nearby, but Bebeha's

An afternoon visitor shares a pot of tea with Bebeha.

neighbour had a grinding stone in her house and would mill small amounts of flour for friends, keeping a little of it in compensation for her labour.

Down below in the courtyard, Roquia was playing with several other children who had come in ones and twos to look for her. Bebeha's large courtyard was a focus for the village children and Roquia often took a central part in their games and activities. Although already a useful worker, she was still a child and easily became absorbed in the games she initiated to amuse the younger children. With loose stones she had outlined a rectangle on the ground to make a play compound and peopled it with little twig dolls dressed with strips of cloth.

While the children were playing, the double wooden doors of the compound opened and a neighbour came in. She was an aunt of Bebeha's, about 60 years old, a widow who lived across the river in her son's house. Especially in summer, when she could easily wade across the river, she often called on Bebeha. Today she wanted to consult her about the approaching wedding of one of the boys in her own family.

Bebeha welcomed her aunt with affection and respect. She made some green tea, which they drank without

milk—unlike the strong black brew laced with buffalo milk that had started the day. Redwanullah scrambled on to the visitor's lap and sat there while the women discussed the problem and came to a tentative conclusion: a piece of cloth with which to make a quilt should be bought in Peshawar as a contribution to the gifts for the bride; and Bebeha would arrange with Shams-ud Din to make the purchase next time he went to the city.

Not long after Bebeha's aunt had left, the doors opened again and Shams-ud Din and Ihsanullah came in. They carried two large baskets filled with their purchases— from sandals to sweetmeats—which they laid on the charpoys under the tree. They then went to find Farman at the *hujra* to discuss which field should be harvested next, while the women prepared supper. Farman's wife had prepared the dough for the bread during the afternoon, and now she hastily shaped the loaves and put them into the oven. While they were cooking, Bebeha walked down to the river to fetch water for the animals and for washing clothes the next day. She swilled out the two earthenware pots she carried and refilled them, then carried them back with her through the rapidly darkening evening. Inside the compound, shadows had gathered in the corners and the flames of the cooking fire cast a flickering light.

By the time the men returned from the *hujra* at 6 p.m., the charpoys had been rearranged to provide seats for everyone, the table was spread with dishes and Bebeha had milked the two buffaloes. The daughters-in-law hovered about serving food: bread, curds of buffalo milk, potatoes in curry sauce, and green tea. The children and younger women stayed in the background until the men had finished eating; then they joined Bebeha at the table to take their own supper.

When all had finished, Ihsanullah fetched the baskets of goods purchased in the Peshawar bazaar. He showed his wife some cloth they had bought at her request and he described another pattern they had considered but rejected. Shams-ud Din sat on a porch step with his arm affectionately round Roquia, watching as Bebeha critically tried on the sandals he had brought her. During the evening, several other relatives slipped in through the door to listen to the conversation. One of Ihsanullah's wife's brothers came for a short while but he soon left again, saying that he was going to sleep, even if they were all mad enough to stay up this late to talk. It was all of 9 p.m. Everyone teased his sister good-humouredly, telling her to tuck him in with the children, and much laughter and joking sounded in the dark courtyard.

At last, one by one, the men and the visitors from other households disappeared to seek their beds. The children had already pulled their quilts over themselves and were sleeping quietly. The women cleared everything away, picking their way over the ground littered with the accumulated debris of the day. A little cry came from Ihsanullah's baby, by now installed again in her pendant cradle under the porch. Her mother rose to fetch her into bed to feed, and half an hour later the mother's dark figure could be seen silently passing in front of the collapsing embers of the fire as she settled the baby back in the cradle.

Last of all, Bebeha moved round the courtyard, her kerosene lantern making a point of yellow light in the soft darkness as she checked that the animals were comfortable and the double doors securely bolted. Then she too lay down and slept. A dog barked in the shrouded village; another answered it. It was just after 10 o'clock.

The cooking fire sheds light on the preparations for supper.

A Hard-Won Livelihood

Pathans have always had a fierce attachment to their land. In the past, the arid mountain country of the Frontier supported few crops and the acreage a man owned contributed more to his honour than his income. For their livelihood, the tribesmen centuries ago turned to raiding and brigandage: the rugged hills made fine natural fortresses and thus gave their territory a value far greater than its meagre harvest merited.

In recent years, however, irrigation has introduced an alternative way of life to banditry. As a result, ploughs have replaced rifles as a prime means of subsistence and tribesmen can earn a modest living from their once

Chaff flies as two Kado men winnow wheat during the harvest. As each field ripens in May, its owner's relatives rally to help gather the crop. The men

infertile fields. Although the menfolk still rate honour above affluence, and conversation above tillage, the villagers of Kado have learnt to exploit their land and its water for all the combination can produce.

Wheat provides the bread that is the basis of the austere Pathan diet; a few fish are netted in the seasonal rivers; and sheep, goats and cattle yield a little milk. Most arable land, however, is turned over to the cash crops of sugar-cane and opium poppies, whose harvest can be traded for tea and soap, for clothing and crockery—and for the expensive weapons that, even on a peaceful Frontier, no tribesman would willingly be without.

do most of the labour; the women help out when necessary, keeping their veils ready for use should they encounter males who are not close kinsmen.

98

A villager casts a fishing net in the shallows
of the Kabul river. In Frontier streams,
fish are too scarce to provide a livelihood,
but even a small catch makes a welcome
addition to the basic family diet of bread.

Discreetly veiled against the eyes of strangers, a woman moves through a field of opium poppies at harvest time. Opium cultivation is illegal in Pakistan: only in the Pathan tribal territories, where no government regulations are enforced, is the narcotic plant grown without restriction.

he was unconcerned that, strictly speaking, he was landless and without a home of his own. "I will own nothing until my father dies," he told me. "If I need money, I must ask my father for some. Meanwhile, I work with the whole family, and am fed and clothed from what we grow and sell as a family. We live together—so why should I need to own anything separately?"

This is not to suggest that Pathans have a completely cavalier attitude towards ownership. Fundamentally, the male Pathan is passionately possessive about three things: his women, his land and his rifle. Of these, women are the most jealously guarded, but land is the most precious—land means independence. Land is by far the most common cause of disputes and most of Kado's outlaws owed their quarrels to land. Indeed, the only time I ever saw Shams-ud Din really angry was when he believed one of his cousins was trying to hold on to some land that he had loaned him temporarily as a favour.

An old Mohmand tale illustrates the general hunger for land. An elder who had owned many fertile acres lay dying. As the old man's last breath drew near, the Angel of Death appeared, carrying a book in which were listed the names of all those entitled to enter Paradise. "Tell me your name," commanded the angel, "and I will consult my book."

"I have been expecting you," responded the elder. "Tell me, Holy One, is there any good land I can buy in Paradise?"

The angel repeated his question.

"Of course," the old Mohmand continued, "if there is no good land in Paradise I could always buy some poor land and improve it."

Again the angel asked for his name.

"Or I would be happy to rent some good land," the elder suggested.

"Your name!" demanded the increasingly irritated angel.

"I could even reconcile myself to renting some bad land."

"Your name!"

Finally, with his dying breath, the old Mohmand begged: "Oh Holy One, if you have nothing else, you must surely have a little land I could sharecrop."

The Mohmand passion for owning land is natural enough nowadays when tribesmen rely on agriculture for their living. But they were no less fanatical about landownership when the entire valley of Kado lacked irrigation and was as desiccated as the surrounding mountains. The brown, infertile soil brought as much honour to the tribesmen who possessed it as today's fields of green and gold, and they treasured every square yard.

Many people of Kado looked back with nostalgia to those days, when the barrenness of the land had led them to seek a living in banditry. It had been a hard life, but their ancestors had been recognized as the scourge of the Peshawar valley, and the old ways still appealed to their warlike nature. Moreover, they could justify their past behaviour on grounds other than sheer love of loot. "It was important to keep control over our area from the lands of unbelievers," Shams-ud Din said. "When we attacked the Hindu merchants of the plains, it was not only for money. It was also for Islam."

Although "the good old days" of armed robbery were over, the men of Kado found a certain stimulation in another illicit occupation a good deal less re-

Young girls prepare fuel made of caked cattle dung. Mixed with straw and water (inset), the dung is shaped into rounds and slapped on to the walls of the compound to harden in the sun. Once dried, it is ready for stoking in a family's hearth or oven.

spectable than sugar refining: the cultivation and smuggling of opium. That they could grow the opium poppy without interference was due to the special status of the tribal territories. In response to international pressure, the Pakistan Government during the 1970s had launched a series of drives to restrict opium production to a few delimited areas, where it was to be grown for pharmaceutical purposes only. The ban was enforced throughout the country, with one notable exception: the Pathan territories of the North-West Frontier Province. Since the government's authority did not extend to the tribal enclaves, the Pathans were able to continue growing opium there. Indeed, they raised production when prices rose following the end of large-scale cultivation in the rest of Pakistan. A field of poppies could produce opium resin worth many times what the same plot would yield if it were planted with sugar-cane. But the Kado villagers, conscious of their proximity to the settled area, were reluctant to devote too much of their land to a crop the government disapproved of so strongly. Even so, in terms of income, the opium poppy became the second most important crop in the village.

A few days after I had watched the cutting of the sugar-cane, I walked across the village to visit Shams-ud Din's cousin Shazar Khan in his small poppy field. I found him alone, surrounded by showers of pink and white petals that had fallen from myriad plants. As a gesture of welcome, he picked up one of the many seed-pods that were lying scattered on the ground, split it open with his fingernails and offered me a handful of the seeds inside it. I knew it was the poppies' resin that provided the opium, but I was uncertain as to the narcotic power of the seeds, so I politely declined. My wariness must have showed, because he burst out laughing and swallowed the handful of seeds himself, to show that they were harmless.

"They are just like biscuits," he said. "We eat them as a snack when working. All the children like them and they do no one any harm." As though to prove his point, my permanent entourage of small boys busily gathered pods from the ground and munched their contents. Reassured, I ate a handful of the tiny seeds. I felt no strange effects; they were spicier than the ordinary poppy seeds Western bakers often scatter on their loaves, but they had the same tendency to lodge irritatingly between my teeth.

The opium itself is extracted only from the pod of the growing poppy plant, but Shazar Khan proudly explained that not a single part of his crop was wasted. After the pods had been milked of their resin, they were split and their seeds taken for food. Then the remnants were boiled to extract the minute traces of opium that remained. The resulting mildly narcotic liquid was administered to children suffering from chest ailments or bad coughs. Even the leaves of the poppy plant were used. Small ones, together with poppy stalks, were saved as fodder and the largest leaves provided a protective wrapping for the opium resin after it had been shaped into small cakes.

Shazar Khan explained that, although no one in Kado smoked opium, a few of the older tribesmen ate small quantities for its narcotic effects; and its use in snuff was widespread. The drug was also used in time of sickness and

Every Sunday, hundreds of animals are driven to Shabkadar market. To attract potential buyers, the owners create eye-catching displays of their livestock. Pathans believe such ornamentation also protects the animals from the evil eye. Some beasts sport a bead collar or gaily coloured scarf; others are hung with bells and pom-poms, or patterned with brilliant vegetable dyes that emphasize the silky sheen of their coats.

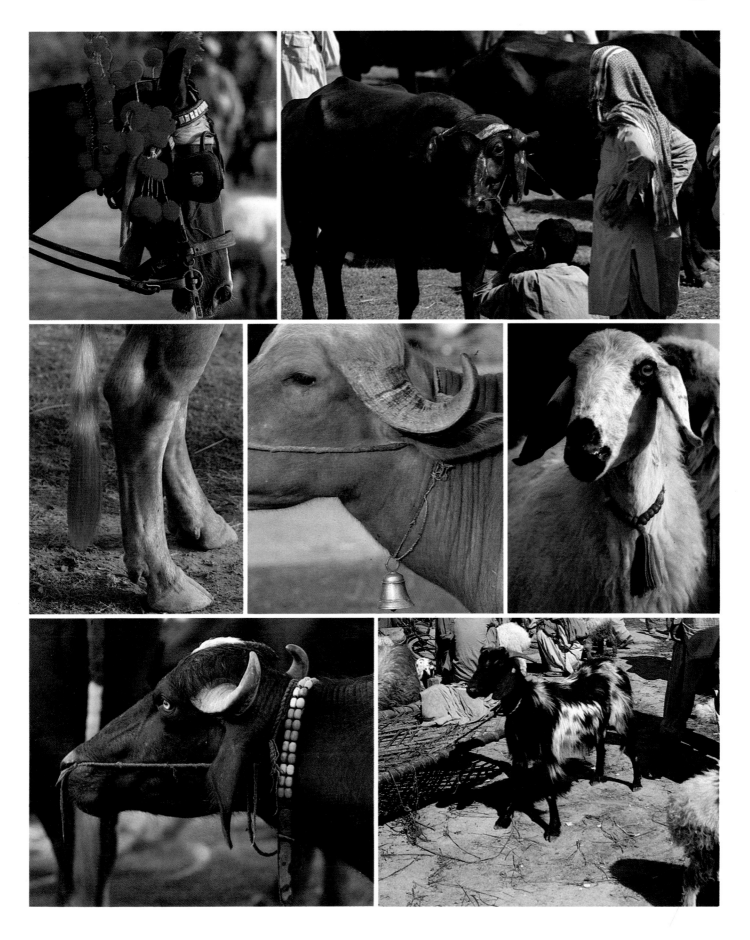

injury to relieve pain. Only a tiny fraction of his opium, however, would be consumed in Kado; he would sell most of it—either in Mian Mandi, a Mohmand market town 10 miles north-west of Kado, or in Landi Kotal, a larger trading centre in Shinwari Pathan territory at the head of the Khyber Pass.

Although opium dealing is not a traditional Pathan occupation (the cultivation of the plants has only been possible since the coming of irrigation), it is perfectly legitimate according to Pathan tribal custom. Shazar Khan, therefore, had no reason to make a secret of his plans. Indeed, two weeks after the harvesting of his resin, he invited me to join him on a visit to Landi Kotal, where he would meet his agent and negotiate a price.

Landi Kotal is only a few miles across the Mohmand Hills from Kado, but the direct route involves crossing rough country and can be made only on foot. Since Shazar Khan had no desire for unnecessary exercise, he arranged at Michni to hire a car and driver, and we made the journey by way of Peshawar. By the time we reached Jamrud fort—the check-point on the border of tribal territory at the approach to the Khyber Pass—the heat of the morning was intense. The guard asked our destination and demanded a toll of a few rupees, which went towards the cost of maintaining the government road. On that occasion, he did not trouble to search us or the car. But according to Shazar Khan, thorough inspections were frequent and so he would never risk carrying opium with him; its discovery would mean a fine or even a jail sentence as well as confiscation.

Landi Kotal's ease of access and its proximity to the Afghan border only a few miles away had made the town a prime smuggling centre. Although it was in tribal territory, its situation on a main road brought it at least partially under the control of the Pakistan Government. However, dealers in both arms and opium seemed to thrive there.

The ascent to Landi Kotal was spectacular. Great peaks towered above us on either side of the pass; and the Peshawar plain, shrouded in mist, stretched out for miles behind. But the town itself was uninviting: a sprawl of mean and dusty streets lined with crumbling buildings spread higgledy-piggledy down a mountainside. We left the car in the care of its driver on the main street. Shazar Khan led us down narrow alley-ways to the bazaar, where armed Pathans jostled around stalls displaying an extraordinary variety of offerings, ranging from the merely unappetizing (slabs of hornet-covered meat) to the downright disreputable (lumps of hashish and automatic rifles).

In the heart of the bazaar, a few yards from the town's central mosque, Shazar Khan stopped before a mud wall, pushed open a large wooden door and ushered me inside. There, we were greeted by a tall, fat Pathan who invited us to sit on wooden boxes and then ordered a boy to bring tea. During the long discussion that followed, our host explained that the current price for opium was low but he expected it to rise later in the year. Like Shams-ud Din's sugar agent, he proposed that he should take immediate delivery and hold the opium for sale at a more favourable time.

So it was agreed. Shazar Khan gave me no hint of the kind of profit he expected to make, which did not surprise me: like all Pathans, he regarded the details of his business dealings as strictly private, and he would have been every bit as discreet had the discussions concerned the sale of an innocuous sugar crop. However, he was obviously satisfied with the meeting. He had re-established his valuable trading contacts in Landi Kotal and now it only remained for him to hire a specialist to smuggle the resin through the Jamrud check-point. Shazar Khan realized, of course, that his agent was merely the first link in a long chain of contacts that would move the opium from Kado to the outside world. What the outside world chose to do with it was of no concern to him, although he must have known that the price he would receive was only a fraction of the opium's ultimate street value on the international market. But the poppy-growers of Kado were content so long as the return from their crops met their own needs.

I noticed that hashish was a common commodity on the streets of Landi Kotal and I wondered why no one in Kado seemed to cultivate it. Ihsanullah explained that wild marijuana plants grew in the Kado area, but few people troubled to gather them because their market value was relatively low and because processing the plants into hashish was too troublesome. Besides, only a few Kado men smoked it regularly.

"No one in my family uses hashish," Ihsanullah once told me. "But I remember that many years ago my father was given some to smoke at a wedding celebration. He said that he felt his end had come, and he had to lie down throughout the festivities. At the time, he imagined that the whole village was gathered round his bed to pray for him and that he was too ill to tell them to go away. He has never touched hashish since that day."

In many respects, I found Pathan village life to be admirably democratic and egalitarian—at least as far as relations among the men were concerned. No Pathan owes allegiance to another; every man is a free agent so long as he does not violate the basic principles of *pukhtunwali* by an action that might be seen to damage the honour of a fellow tribesman. However, one aspect of their tribal code inevitably establishes a measure of social inequality. "The perfect Mohmand," Shams-ud Din once told me, "is one who follows *pukhtunwali* and who has enough land to bring up his family properly." Of course, by that definition many Pathans are less than perfect. Most land is owned by senior-lineage families such as Shams-ud Din's and many junior-lineage families have no land at all. The latter would buy land if they could but, since no Pathan will sell any unless he has to—in settlement of pressing debts, for instance—those who are born landless are likely to remain so. Land-owning Pathans do not discriminate in any way against less fortunate families, but it was obvious to me that a senior-lineage man with a few acres was held in far greater respect than a junior-lineage man with none.

Young Riaz, one of Kado's two shepherd boys, was a good example of a landless villager. He was paid by local farmers to escort their livestock to meagre grazing in the mountains. Every day this lean 14-year-old set off before dawn with 20 or more goats and returned them to the courtyards of their owners in late afternoon. He wore the same loose clothes and turban as other villagers and he carried his daily supplies—bread, salt, onion and a skin container of water—in a cloth-wrapped bundle slung on his belt. As he walked, he played haunting little tunes on a flute.

One morning, I accompanied Riaz out of the village with the goats. As the sun peeped over the crest of a mountain, he stopped the herd, placed his flute on the ground, and knelt towards Mecca and prayed. Then he rounded up a few goats that had strayed, took up his flute and piped out a tune accompanied by the bleating of his little herd as they moved off through a narrow ravine. It was a scene suspended in time.

But of course, Riaz's pastoral image could not be equated with traditional Pathanhood. Possessing neither a rifle nor land to defend, he lacked the independence to which all tribesmen aspired. With time, he might be able to save enough money to buy himself a weapon, but he would probably have to spend the rest of his life working for others. Since no senior-lineage family would give a daughter away to a landless man, his chances of improving his lot by marriage would be small. His best hopes for advancement lay in the general economic development of the area, which promised an all-round increase in prosperity. And he could always leave the tribal lands altogether to seek better prospects in the outside world.

The route of exile has been a high-road to fortune for many Pathans. They are a vigorous, self-reliant people, and those who have left the tribal areas and joined the mainstream of Pakistani society often reach high positions in business and government. Not surprisingly, many tribesmen choose to follow a military career, and at least two contemporary heads of state—Ayub Khan and Yahya Khan—could claim Pathan ancestry. But within the confines of the tribal territories the code of conduct has a restrictive effect, and those who need to accumulate wealth to buy land are often unable to seek profitable occupations without involving themselves in work considered demeaning for a self-respecting tribesman. For example, it is acceptable for a landless Mohmand to work on another's land or to herd the village's cattle for a living; some Kado men had even gone to work in the oil-rich Islamic states of the Persian Gulf, from where they sent back money to their families. But there are other occupations that it would be quite unthinkable for any tribal Pathan to turn himself to.

Kado had a barber, a carpenter and a blacksmith, all of whom were essential to the everyday life of the village. However, these occupations were left to non-Pathans: less prideful people who belonged to unrelated but associated tribes that had migrated to the Kado area with their Mohmand hosts centuries before. The demarcation came about because the Mohmand men spent too much time in warfare and in feuding to attend to these tasks themselves. Over time, the two tribal groups have retained their separate identities: the Pathans are as devoted to *pukhtunwali* as ever, while the service groups follow the less demanding routines of the trades that have become theirs.

Although the Pathans do not intermarry with them, the co-existence is comfortable and the village craftsmen's position is by no means one of oppressed inferiority. These workers are certainly not economically inferior. Indeed,

Their camels heavily laden with firewood, tents and baggage, nomad Pathans cross a hillside above Kado on their way to spring pastures among the mountains of Afghanistan. The nomads descend to the Peshawar plain at the start of each winter in search of sheltered sites for their camps and grazing for their livestock.

some of them make a relatively handsome living as indispensable servants of Pathan communities. A carpenter, for example, is often one of the richest men in a Pathan village. Landholders rely upon him to make and repair their farming implements, and to maintain their sugar-cane pressing-machines. He also makes beds, doors, window-frames and beams for houses. He is responsible for constructing the charpoy on which every Pathan bridegroom sits during his marriage ceremony, and for shaping the wooden board on which every Pathan is eventually carried to his grave.

The barber is equally indispensable. His duties extend far beyond giving routine shaves and hair-cuts. He plays a part in most important rituals: performing circumcisions, delivering wedding invitations and making a written record of all gifts to the bridegroom so that they may be reciprocated on a similar occasion. He shaves and manicures the corpse before a funeral and, with the carpenter's assistance, generally acts as the village undertaker.

One afternoon, Ihsanullah introduced me to a pair of these craftsmen, the brothers Alam and Mohammed Gul, who had established a thriving family business in Kado by combining the roles of blacksmith and carpenter. We found them resting on the usual charpoys in a clearing of beaten earth that resembled the *hujra* of Shams-ud Din. In the centre of the area was a small stone forge. Since the forge was cold, I used it as a seat. At once Alam Gul began gesticulating angrily towards me and, for the first time in Kado, I felt positively unwelcome. Then Ihsanullah came over and asked me if I would mind getting up. "Alam is not angry with you, but he is very worried because he believes that anyone who sits on his forge will get smallpox." It seemed a bizarre superstition. I suspected that Alam had invented it himself to protect his none-too-solidly constructed forge—his source of livelihood—from

A tribesman has his armpits shaved by the village barber, who also performs ceremonial duties, including funeral rites and circumcisions, for which each villager pays him an annual fee. Although the post makes a barber relatively prosperous, Pathans look down on him because he does not follow the tribal code: he carries no gun and he depends on others for his livelihood.

careless visitors such as myself. In any event, I leapt from my perch murmuring an apology that changed the scowls on the brothers' faces into smiles.

There was little sign of industry from either of the brothers when we arrived; but soon afterwards, at four o'clock, the customers began to arrive: a steady stream of villagers carrying ploughs, knives, wooden bedposts and a variety of kitchen utensils, all in need of repair. A fire of brushwood and caked dung was set alight in the forge and kept aglow with bellows operated by Mohammed Gul's teenage son. Mohammed himself began heating the twisted blade of a plough. Meanwhile, his brother began to mend a broken wooden spoon. Soon, their faces gleamed with sweat.

"They are usually busy at this time," Ihsanullah told me. "Every day they start work here after the sun loses its heat. At other times they can be asked to visit a house to carry out some task. My family always gives them a share of the harvest and in return they agree to serve us all the year round."

In dress, religion, manner and speech, the craftsmen of Kado seemed the same as the Mohmand tribesmen. They had the same family-based lifestyle and they kept their women in the same strict purdah as did the Pathans. Some even owned small plots of land, which they cultivated in addition to practising their crafts. How then could they be regarded as unequal?

Ihsanullah dismissed my question with something akin to puzzlement. "It is impossible to be equal to a Pathan if you are not a Pathan," he declared. "These people do not follow our code. They do not carry guns and they take no part in feuds or fighting. They are good people, but they are not Pathans; they exist only to serve us."

That the servants might be wealthier than the masters was irrelevant. For Ihsanullah, as for all Pathans, wealth is only the means to an end. The end itself is the freedom to follow *pukhtunwali*; and between the code's adherents and lesser men who live by different laws is an immense gulf. Even the poorest of Pathans, scratching a living from rocky soil, in threadbare clothing with an old, worn-out rifle slung from his shoulder, cherishes the knowledge that there is not enough money in the world to bridge that great divide.

Five | **A Pervasive Pattern of Belief**

On an evening in mid-August in the town of Shabkadar, in the Pathan tribal area, a revered *mullah*—the nearest Islamic equivalent to a priest—made an important declaration. Since 11 witnesses had now come to him claiming they had seen the new moon, he was, in accordance with Koranic doctrine, officially announcing the end locally of the month-long fast of Ramadan; the annual festival of celebration could begin on the following day. His message spread by word of mouth to most of the Mohmand tribal villages, including Kado, where it was greeted with great pleasure—not least, I was told, because the *mullah's* decision allowed the village to celebrate before the rest of Pakistan could. In the settled area, the government had already announced that the end of Ramadan would be a day later.

In expectation of the *mullah's* announcement, excitement had been building up in Kado during the day, which to my hosts was the 29th of Ramadan—the ninth and holiest of the Muslim months, during which the Koran is said to have been handed down by divine revelation. (The Muslim year is divided into 12 lunar months and has only 354 days, with the result that every 33 Muslim years are approximately equal to 32 of our solar years; and each Muslim month moves through the seasons rather than remaining insepar- ably identified with a particular time of summer or winter.)

The Mohmands, who accept the code of Islam as unquestioningly as they do the code of *pukhtunwali*, strictly obey the rules of the fast. Throughout the month of Ramadan, between sunrise and sunset no food or water passes the lips of any adult; nor are the men permitted to smoke or take snuff. Up to the age of puberty, children are exempt from fasting, as are pregnant women and the sick. After sunset, abstaining from food is expressly forbidden; one must eat something as soon as the sun goes down, even if it is only a date. Still, the daylight hours of hunger and thirst in the intense heat are not only generally exhausting but depressing. Thus, the appearance of the new moon marking

the end of their ordeal is one of the most eagerly awaited events of the year.

Observing the fast of Ramadan is one of the five Pillars of Islam. According to the Prophet Muhammad, "The foul smell of the faster's mouth is sweeter before God than the scent of musk." Most Mohmands are strict observers of the other four pillars: the creed that "there is no god but Allah and Muhammad is His Prophet"; the saying of prayers five times a day; the giving to the poor of one fortieth part of one's annual savings and, for those who can afford the cost, a pilgrimage to Mecca. Many Mohmands would add, as an unofficial sixth pillar, the obligation of waging holy war against unbelievers.

When Ramadan falls in high summer, as it did during my stay in Kado, it puts an especially severe strain on the most even of tempers. The British explorer Sir Richard Burton, who once made a pilgrimage to Mecca disguised as a Pathan, spent the summer Ramadan of 1855 in Cairo and minced no words in describing the experience. "The chief effect of the 'blessed month' upon the True Believers," he wrote, "is to darken their tempers into positive gloom. The men curse one another and beat the women. The women slap and abuse the children, and those in their turn cruelly entreat, and use bad language to, the dogs and cats. You can scarcely spend ten minutes in any populous part of the city without hearing some violent dispute. The Mosques are crowded with a sulky, grumbling population, making themselves offensive to one another whilst working their way to heaven."

In the easy-going *hujras* of Kado I was struck not so much by the tense atmosphere during Ramadan as by the relief that followed it. The festival held on the first day of the following month, Shawwal, is the liveliest of the Mohmand year, and when I was in Kado Shams-ud Din decided he would make the day especially memorable by slaughtering a buffalo. He intended only his closest friends and relatives to share this bounty with his family, so he sent out written invitations to the chosen ones: "We will be pleased if you would come for a meal at 8 to 9 o'clock in the morning tomorrow." But inevitably, word got round. The whole village showed up for the feast—and such are the laws of hospitality that it was out of the question for Shams-ud Din to turn anyone away. He ended up distributing the food to at least twice as many people as he had intended.

All the guests, who had first gone to the village mosque to pray, appeared in high spirits. They attacked their food, drink and snuff with relish, chattering animatedly. Within a few days, their old disputes would resurface and their rifles would reappear on their shoulders; but for the moment the influence of Ramadan was strong and each man felt at peace with his neighbours.

The word Islam means submission—to God, not man. The tribesmen have no difficulty reconciling Koranic doctrine with their independent ways. As good Muslims, the Pathans submit themselves to the will of Allah in everything they do. They have no separate compartment for religion: to them, Islam is a force that informs and animates every aspect of their lives.

This suffusion of belief goes far deeper than the so-called five pillars, which represent no more than its outward manifestation. Obviously, major rituals such as weddings, funerals and the circumcision that marks a boy's entry into his religion are conducted according to strict Islamic precept. Less formally, the Pathan attitude to sickness and health, to misfortune and to happiness, is part of the same system of faith. As I discovered during my stay in Kado, prayers are an invariable first recourse in time of trouble.

If prayers fail, they are followed frequently by practices that seem quite close to witchcraft, at least to Western eyes. For example, the burning of Koranic verses with muttered imprecations is an expedient frequently used to ward off illness. For Pathans, of course, such behaviour is a perfectly logical act of faith. In any case, the Koran and the reported sayings of the Prophet Muhammad provide them with justification for most of their actions. To take one instance, Muhammad himself approved the use of spells to protect against the workings of the evil eye. Even when no such clear authority exists, Pathans are so sure of their status as true believers that they piously claim that everything they do is founded on Islamic principle.

Islam's lack of a clear, central authority to clarify doctrine helps to encourage the Pathan attitude. Just as Pathan tribal society has no regular system of government, so Islam has no ecclesiastical hierarchy. The many *mullahs* in the tribal territory are not appointed by official authority. Instead, they form a craft guild of sorts: sons follow their fathers in their calling. A young man may spend some time at a special religious school, and when he is old enough he will usually be apprenticed to a holy man located in another village. His apprenticeship continues until death creates a vacancy in the area. Failing such an opportunity, he returns home to act as a second-in-command to his father, or he may even become an itinerant, wandering until he finds a community that requires his services.

The *mullah*'s tasks are to care for the local mosque, to provide basic religious instruction for the children and generally to attend to the spiritual needs of

Inside a Kado compound women prostrate
themselves and bow their heads in prayer.
Communal services are held by Muslims
every Friday, but local Islamic custom
forbids women to join the men in the mosque.
Instead, they congregate in a courtyard.

his congregation. The whole system is highly informal, and the *mullahs* must rely for their authority largely on the esteem the tribesmen hold for wisdom and for those who follow a religious life. That esteem is not always unreserved: Pathans are quite capable of dismissing an old, illiterate *mullah* as an ignorant and interfering fool.

Not even the most respected of *mullahs* can levy any kind of tithe, since that would imply an authority offensive to most tribesmen. In a few cases, villagers voluntarily give a percentage of their crops to an especially cherished holy man, but usually a village *mullah* lives by farming a small area of land set aside by the community for the mosque. If the *mullah* is a member of the local tribe, he may also farm land of his own. Few *mullahs*, though, belong to any Pathan tribe; and none of the three who served Kado's two mosques and 70 households was a Pathan. The *mullahs* of Kado provided a good cross-section of their profession. The main mosque was the domain of an ailing father and his son; the son was well educated and, although not yet 30, he had taken full charge. He had also gained the trust of most of the village—a remarkable achievement for so young a man. The other mosque, a much smaller building in old Kado, was run by an aged *mullah* nearing his dotage, who had lost most of his congregation to the more energetic younger man.

There are other Islamic holy men who do not generally participate in the ritual of the mosques. Some, known simply as *pirs*, meaning pious men, are wandering preachers who make their living from the gifts of the faithful. The Pathans tell a story, possibly apocryphal, of a *pir* who visited the Afridi Pathans a century ago. The preacher berated them for their godlessness and lack of respect for the holy men of Islam: "I have travelled your land for many days and not once have I seen a shrine where rest the bones of a holy man; not a single saint's tomb for the people to pray at. You are a disgrace to Islam." The Afridis had to agree and decided to rectify the situation. They shot the *pir*, built him a marvellous tomb and ever after came there to pray.

Holy men who attain sufficient celebrity are often graced with the title of sheikh. Near Kado, for example, is the shrine of Sheikh Foulad Baba, a holy man who died early in this century. His four elderly grandsons still look after the shrine, which is reputed to be of special efficacy in curing smallpox. Villagers go there with those who are already sick and they also bring children who, they hope, will acquire immunity from the disease.

A visit to a shrine is one of the few occasions when a Pathan woman will leave the confines of her village, as Shams-ud Din's wife Bebeha did when, accompanied by her daughters-in-law, she went to the shrine of Foulad Baba to pray with them for the protection of her oldest grandson. The boy was especially dear to his family because he had been born to Ihsanullah only after four childless years of marriage and as yet had no brothers; although the child was hale enough, Bebeha's joy in him was constantly tempered with anxieties over his safety and health. With Ihsanullah, I followed the three heavily veiled women at a discreet distance. The shrine, a small stone building with an arched roof containing the holy man's tomb, was marked by numerous small flags and bright scraps of cloth hanging from sticks set in

the surrounding earth. The pieces of cloth, Ihsanullah explained, were offerings that supplicants had made to the sheikh. As she reached the shrine, Bebeha pulled a scrap of cloth from beneath her *burqa*, tied it to one of the sticks and with her two companions entered the building to pray.

In the shade of a gnarled fig tree just outside the shrine sat an old, white-bearded man—one of the grandsons of Sheikh Foulad Baba. Through Ihsanullah, I asked him to what the shrine owed its powers and he described to us in a matter-of-fact way the miracles attributed to his grandfather.

Foulad Baba was born in Shabkadar, the son of a holy man who kept buffaloes for a living. When Foulad Baba was only eight years old, he had the power to order the buffaloes to sleep or wake. At the age of 20, he was asked to help the people of a nearby town who were afflicted by an epidemic of smallpox. Foulad Baba prayed there and the disease went away. After that miracle, Foulad decided to retire into solitude to strengthen his mystic powers. He began his journey to the place where the shrine now stands. On the way, a boatman refused to convey him across a river. Undaunted, the sheikh struck the water with his rod and waited until the river dried up. Word spread and people came from many villages to visit the holy man. Eventually, he died and was buried on the spot where we now stood. But even then the miracles did not stop.

"You see those three large stones lying there?" asked Foulad's grandson. "Once some robbers were chasing three women near the tomb. The women called out for the sheikh and God to save their chastity, and they were saved by being turned to stones—those stones over there."

Other shrines near Kado had specialities of their own. Probably the most important to the villagers was a shrine near Shabkadar, visited to counter the

As dawn breaks over the hills behind the village of Kado, a goatherder kneels in prayer, facing Mecca while his flock grazes on a stony pasture. Five times daily—at daybreak, noon, mid-afternoon, sunset and after nightfall—devout Muslims interrupt their work or leisure to worship.

effects of the evil eye, a concern that was something of a local obsession. I knew that the evil eye was blamed for many misfortunes, but at first I did not understand exactly how it was believed to operate. "Suppose you owned a beautiful bullock," expounded Ihsanullah, "and one day a man came up to you and said, 'You have a beautiful bullock.' If half an hour later the bullock went lame or got cut on a sharp rock, then the man who praised the bullock obviously had the evil eye."

The evil eye, Ihsanullah continued, had nothing to do with ill will. It was, he said, a malevolent force that descended seemingly at random, using innocent Mohmands only as vehicles: no blame attached to a man thought to have the affliction. Instead, to lift the curse his fellow villagers helped him with prayers and spells. He himself would seek the aid of the *mullah* and, if necessary, pay a visit to an appropriate shrine.

To annul the effects of the evil eye, the people of Kado relied on a variety of counter-charms in addition to prayers. If the person with the evil eye was unidentified, the tribesmen would collect the leaves of various herbs, dry them and burn them; the smoke was believed to help undo the harm the evil eye had caused. If the culprit was known, he or she would strengthen the countermeasure by contributing some token possession—such as a hair, or a thread from a garment—to the burning leaves.

However, prevention was reckoned to be better than cure, so most villagers observed some elementary precautions. Newly built houses, considered especially likely to attract the evil eye, were always guarded by scarecrow-like dolls, animal skulls or black flags; these were believed capable of diverting the eye's attention from the house and those who would live there.

It was not only in the curing of supernaturally inspired ailments that Pathan religious practice seemed to verge on the occult. Everyday medicine, also seen as a province of Islam, had its own forms of wizardry. Sickness, in fact, is not common among the Pathans: infant mortality is high, but those who survive childhood—and who avoid the bullets of an avenging enemy—generally live on into a tough and wiry old age. Given the kind of treatment I saw meted out in Kado, such toughness was a vital asset.

A cold cure that Shams-ud Din's grandson had to endure, for example, seemed at least as unpleasant as his malady. The incident took place out of sight inside the compound; but, according to Toby, the mother had taken a freshly killed chicken, skinned it and tied the skin, with the feathers still in place, round the protesting infant's head. The child's discomfort increased when his grandmother pushed a stick rubbed with ash into his mouth and pressed it on his tongue. No one was able to explain how this cure worked, except to say that, among other things, the ash brought up phlegm.

For a more serious illness or complaint, such as cholera, Shams-ud Din explained that they would rub a raw egg on top of the victim's head and tie the chicken skin round his body. For most fevers, a fresh goatskin or calfskin would be wrapped round the unfortunate patient's body—"to draw out the heat". For a stomach ache, though, the sufferer would receive a more com-

An old midwife renowned for her healing powers treats a backache. To effect the cure, verses from the Koran inscribed on pieces of paper are thrown into a clay bowl and set alight; the hot bowl is then placed upside down over a circle of bread dough pressed on the sufferer's most painful spot.

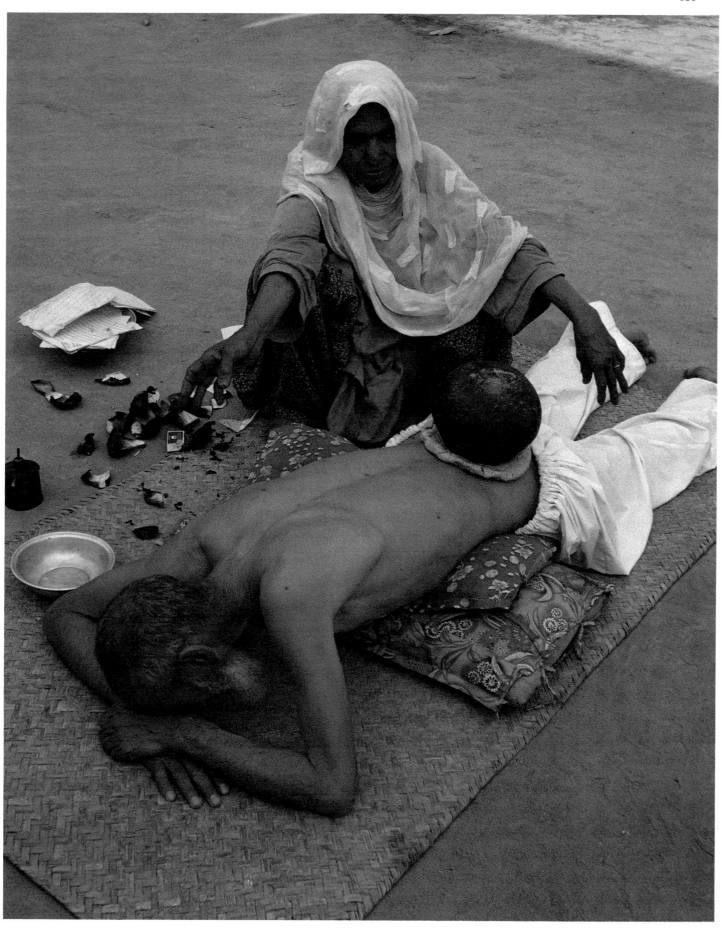

prehensible treatment: he would be fed a hot syrup made from sugar, milk and the aromatic seeds of a small local plant.

Shams-ud Din himself provided an instance of an attempted cure that combined Islamic custom with commonsense folk-medicine. He was plagued with chronic backache and, although the pain was not immobilizing, it flared up during our visit and forced him to seek relief. As he had done on previous occasions, he first consulted a village *mullah*, who wrote down a verse to be placed in a small leather pouch attached to Shams-ud Din's clothes. I had seen many villagers, especially children, wearing such talismans. Now I learnt that particular verses were believed to be effective against particular ailments. For example, a man who had been bitten by a snake might wear the following prayer: "In the name of Allah, the beneficent, the merciful. O black scorpion, O black serpent, reduce the effect of your poison. It is a humble request." Even animals had verses tied round their necks, both to cure existing illnesses and to keep away any that might threaten.

Shams-ud Din was a devout man; but, like the rest of his people, he did not necessarily regard such prayers as an infallible remedy. When his verse-pouch failed to bring about a cure, he sent for an old midwife from Michni. Her normal function was to deliver babies and to care for female complaints in her village and nearby areas; no male doctor is allowed to treat Mohmand women. In addition to her gynaecological lore, she was thought to have magical powers and so was often visited at her home by men as well as women who wanted ailments cured. There was an extra fee for house calls.

Thus she arrived in Kado—an old, stooped figure who had long ago discarded her veil. She instructed Shams-ud Din to take off his shirt and lie on the ground on his stomach. He did so, a little apprehensively.

Producing a lump of dough large enough to make a loaf of bread and kneading it into a flat, circular shape, the midwife vigorously pressed it on to the afflicted area of Shams-ud Din's back. Then she took pieces of paper inscribed with Koranic verses and dropped them into a large clay pot she had brought with her. Muttering and intoning to herself, she set the pieces of paper alight. She then quickly up-ended the pot with its flaming contents and buried the rim in the sheet of dough on Shams-ud Din's back. A few seconds later, she raised the pot, allowing smoke to escape. She tested the dough's heat with her fingers and poked some more papers inscribed with verses into the inverted pot. As they caught light, she pressed the pot into the dough once more. After a fourth repetition, Shams-ud Din began grimacing and told the old woman to desist. Laughing, she obeyed.

Once the dough had been peeled away, I could see that the skin on Shams-ud Din's back had been pulled taut. The process had clearly caused him considerable pain. Essentially, he had been treated with a hot poultice; the verses that provided the heat had no doubt made their own contribution.

I asked the midwife whether the dough-and-Koran medicine was used on other parts of the body and if it would cure other ills. "Of course it can," was her reply. "But it is most important as a remedy for barren women." When she treated infertility, the midwife explained, she placed the dough on the

A woman watches her grandson to make sure he does not remove the chicken skin tied round his head to cure a cold. A folk remedy often used if prayers fail, the skin and feathers, left in place for about half an hour, are believed to draw out sickness.

belly and recommended that the patient should take complete rest for a week afterwards, eating only heated food.

When the midwife had gone, Shams-ud Din bravely declared that his back was feeling much better. But the cure was short-lived; a few days later he again complained of aches in his back and was ready to try a new treatment. This time, though, he arranged to have his back examined by a trained physician in Peshawar. Unfortunately, the techniques of modern medicine made no more headway than had the nostrums of his ancestors, and when we left Kado he was still complaining.

Shams-ud Din was not the only Mohmand to be disappointed by modern medicine. The history of a strange young villager named Shams-ur Rahman demonstrated that, and also showed another aspect of Islam—the sense of community that it engenders.

Shams-ur Rahman was something of a religious fanatic. Whenever I encountered him, he took me to one side and passionately decried the bad habits and irreligious behaviour of the people of Kado. "They are heathens," he once exclaimed to me, "and Allah will smite them. They pretend to be Muslims, but it is only a pretence. I have seen it all in this picture." At this, he pulled from inside his shirt a piece of Polaroid film that Toby had earlier discarded. The film showed only a confusion of blobs and lines, but somewhere in it Shams-ur Rahman claimed he could see devils watching his people.

I knew how strong was the Mohmands' devotion to Islam, so I was taken aback by his accusations. I was even more surprised by the lack of rebuttal from any bystander who heard his accusations. Eventually, I was told that Shams-ur Rahman was what they called "mental"; not long before, he had suffered a complete nervous breakdown. A sensitive, educated man who had been a schoolteacher by profession, he simply found it impossible to endure the conflict of living in two worlds: the modern, rapidly changing world his education had exposed him to and the static, traditional world of Kado.

Shams-ur Rahman's family had made every effort to cure him. First, they had taken him to see a holy man at a shrine that marked the grave of an unofficial local saint. But several visits failed to produce any improvement. Undeterred, his family then sent him to a clinic in Peshawar, where he had been given electric-shock treatments over a period of nine months. But when this course failed, his family and fellow tribesmen still allowed him living space in Kado society, merely smiling at his eccentricities and ignoring his occasional outbursts. It was God's will that they should bear with him, just as it was God's will that had sent him his affliction in the first place. As a true Islamic community, they would never think of sending him away.

Islam is a deeply conservative religion, but its rituals are rarely elaborate—particularly among Pathans, where poverty discourages ostentatious display. Towards the end of our stay I attended the circumcision of Ihsanullah's 18-month-old son and found that the ritual aspect was a good deal less evident than the surgery itself. Matter-of-fact considerations prevailed. Having made up his mind to have the operation performed, the father summoned the local barber, who arrived promptly carrying his rudimentary equipment. In the family courtyard, which had been vacated for the occasion by all the womenfolk, the barber placed a clay pot on the ground, poured in some water and added a powder that turned the liquid purple—presumably a form of disinfectant. After piling some ash next to the pot, he produced a cut-throat razor. The boy, meanwhile, was playing on the charpoy on which the operation was to take place. Around him, the men of his family disputed who was to hold him when all was ready. They eventually agreed that Shams-ud Din, as the most experienced, should take charge.

The inevitability of the operation made it no less painful to watch. I found myself clenching my teeth as the razor was put to work, causing howls of protest from the infant. The operation was quick and efficient, however. In seconds the cut was made, the purple disinfectant poured on and the ash sprinkled over to stop the bleeding. The men made loud congratulatory noises and tried to distract the infant with sweets and money, while the barber wrapped the tiny piece of cut-off tissue in a cloth and tied it to the child's ankle, where it was to remain for a few days as evidence that the ritual had been performed. The baby was still howling—although he had been given a light sedative dose of opium, it had evidently not yet taken effect.

Eventually the barber was paid and left. The child, his body covered with a fine cloth, went to sleep next to the new, beautifully illustrated Koran with which he had been presented to mark the occasion. The rest of us allowed the courtyard to be reoccupied by the women and settled down again in the masculine tranquillity of the hujra, where we could talk over the event.

Several of the men remembered when circumcision was a more elaborate ceremony. "In the past," I was told, "the boys were mounted on horses before the operation and led to the house of a holy man, who prayed for them."

Whether circumcision was treated as a surgical operation or an occasion for ceremony, it was always arranged in advance. By its very nature, a funeral cannot be, and we found that the Mohmand rites of death and burial were both stark and simple. Soon after our arrival in Kado, our morbid hope—common to anthropologists and the endlessly curious—of seeing a funeral was abruptly fulfilled. Within hours of each other, two women died in the village. The first was an unexpected and tragic case: a young woman who died in childbirth, leaving a baby daughter. "At least it was good that the baby lived," I commented to Ihsanullah. "No", was his reply. "It was bad. The baby has no mother and will be a burden on her mother's sister." Among Pathans, large families are liked; many sons are ideal; but to be a motherless daughter is a bad beginning to life in a Mohmand village.

Meanwhile, an elderly woman was dying in another household, and Toby was taken by Bebeha to see her. The woman lay on a charpoy in a small dark room crowded with women. A relative, about 60 years old, crouched beside her, shooing flies away from the woman's shrunken face and the open mouth through which she breathed faintly. Her small hands, like those of a child, moved aimlessly or groped for the quilt that covered her. A younger woman at the foot of the charpoy unwrapped a Koran covered by a flower-patterned cloth and read verses from it while the other women joined in or cried softly.

Bebeha prayed, went over to the charpoy, consoled the elderly relative and checked the pulse in the old woman's throat. Another old woman, sitting on the floor, was fanning the patient's face with a mulberry branch. Suddenly she stopped fanning and nodded. A wail came from the relative standing by the charpoy, and all the women began to cry aloud. Toby, who was standing against a wall at the back of the room, saw a man—the dead woman's son—rush through the door, push his way through his sobbing female relatives and throw himself at his mother's feet, crying loudly "Mother! Mother!" His younger brother followed and led him away. Bebeha took Toby outside to where I waited, so she saw none of the obsequies that followed.

From where we stood, we could also hear the keening of female voices from the compound just a few hundred yards away where the young woman had died; the sound was in eerie harmony with the lamentations from close by. In that other household, the preparations for the funeral would be almost complete: in the hot climate of the Frontier Province the interval between death and burial was rarely more than a few hours. In that space of time, the rites prescribed by Islamic tradition would be performed. A cloth would be tied round the corpse's head to keep the jaw closed, and close relatives would pay their respects and take a last look at the deceased's unveiled face. Then the body would be undressed and ritually washed—a dead woman by women, a dead man by men. Finally, it would be shrouded for the grave in a muslin sheet. The clothes would be set aside and, with the rest of the deceased's wardrobe, would be donated to a *mullah* for the poor of the village.

A few days before, I had presented Shams-ud Din and his brother with two fine muslin sleeping bags. They were intended as a welcome alternative to the simple sheets Pathan sleepers usually wrapped round themselves. I had sensed that the two men were unhappy about accepting the gifts, but could not fathom the reason until Ihsanullah finally asked me why I was giving them each a death shroud. Now, as I watched the covered body of the young woman being brought out of her courtyard on a wide wooden plank set on a charpoy, I could not help but speculate that my sleeping bags had been given to her family and put to practical use.

The funeral cortège consisted only of men; the women remained weeping in their compounds. Four relatives carried the body on its charpoy and the other men of the village followed behind, weaving among the compounds until they reached the edge of Kado, where they stopped to offer funeral prayers read by the young *mullah* from the main village mosque. We had been told by Shams-ud Din that there would be no objection to our attending the funeral, but many of the men were obviously hostile to our presence, so we kept a respectful distance as we followed at the rear of the procession.

The men moved at a smart pace until they reached the graveyard at the edge of the village. Here, a trench approximately five feet deep had been dug on a north-south axis. At the bottom of the trench a space had been hollowed out along the length of the west side. The woman's body was placed on its side in this space, with her head resting on a pillow of sand and facing west to-

A cloth doll stands next to a black flag atop a newly built house. Both the figure and the flag are believed to draw the attention of the evil eye away from the new house and its inhabitants, and thus avert bad luck.

A fairground salesman relies on his python to draw an attentive crowd. Attracted by his snake-handling skills, the showman's audience stays long enough to hear him extol the all-purpose curative powers of the home-made ointment he hopes to sell.

Pathan children stare in fascinated horror as the pitchman offers them a close look at his captive python. While he performs, his assistant is busy peddling the remedy to the children's equally enthralled parents.

Young Pathan men gamble on a local version of a roulette wheel that uses stylized animal pictures in place of numbers. Although the stakes are usually small, the gamesters invite the disapproval of their more devout elders: betting is forbidden by Islam.

Children look on in puzzlement as two dice players place their stakes on a garishly coloured carpet whose patterns correspond to the markings on each die. The gambling is run by city dwellers from Peshawar, who find it easy to gull the tribal Pathan men.

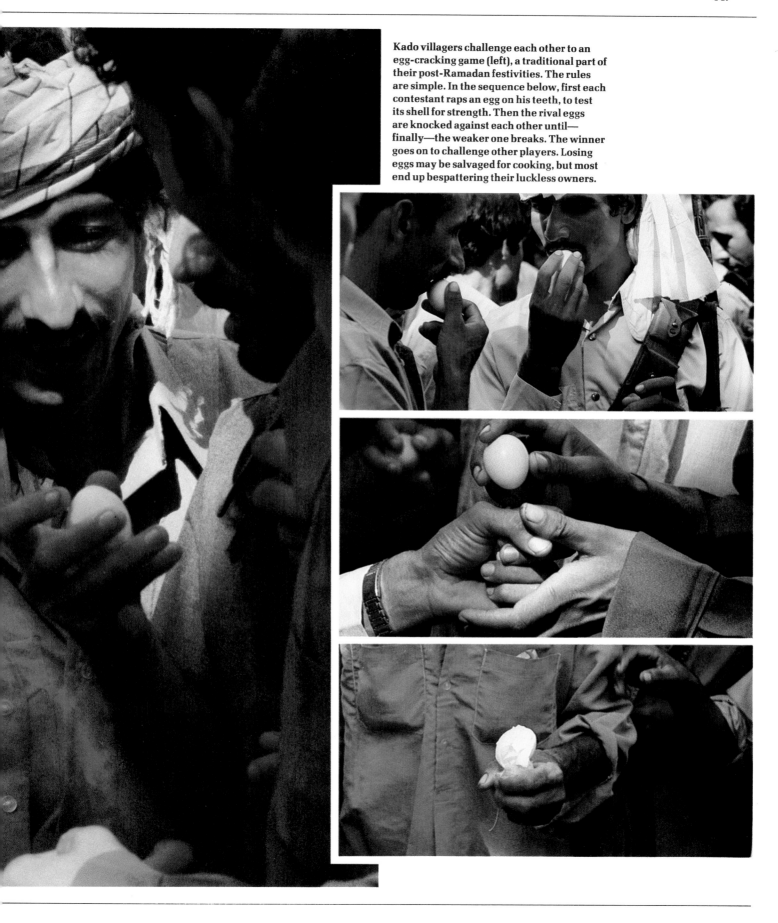

Kado villagers challenge each other to an egg-cracking game (left), a traditional part of their post-Ramadan festivities. The rules are simple. In the sequence below, first each contestant raps an egg on his teeth, to test its shell for strength. Then the rival eggs are knocked against each other until—finally—the weaker one breaks. The winner goes on to challenge other players. Losing eggs may be salvaged for cooking, but most end up bespattering their luckless owners.

Watched by tribesmen who have wagered on the contest, a fighting cock rears back preparing to strike at its opponent. The struggle will be bloody, but the birds are too valuable to be allowed to fight to the death. The loser's owner will retrieve his battered fighting cock before the victor can kill it.

Six | **Dispensing a Simple Justice**

One Friday evening, after discussion with other senior villagers, Shams-ud Din approached me with a formal invitation. "We are holding a *jirga* tomorrow," he declared. "The elders are to assemble in the *hujra* of Nur Rahman. The session may last all day. A father and son in Kado have been arguing about money and we are hoping to settle their dispute peacefully. We have agreed that you may be present, to see Pathan justice at work."

It was news I had been hoping to hear. I had known for some time that a *jirga* was imminent; Shams-ud Din had hinted as much weeks before and for the past few days the conversation of the men in the village had been devoted to little else. But our time in Kado was drawing to a close and I had feared that I might have to leave without seeing in action the tribal council that exercises the only administrative authority Pathans recognize.

It was hard to imagine them accepting any authority. From endless hours of *hujra* talk, I had learnt the value they placed on a man's independence and the contempt they felt for those who allowed themselves to be pressured by others. Again and again, tribesmen expounding on their favourite subject— *pukhtunwali*—would sum up with the phrase: "Every man is a *malik*."

Malik is the Arab word for king, and Pathans fondly cherish the belief that the Prophet Muhammad was so pleased with them as a group that he conferred the title on each one of them. With time, the meaning of the word decayed into something closer to chieftain than king, but the concept—that all Pathans are not only equal but are so at an exalted level—has, if anything, become more firmly rooted. Any Pathan head of household, if asked the question "Who is the *malik*?", would reply without hesitation: "I am."

A way of life that allows such freedom to the individual is close to anarchy and not all observers have been moved to admiration by it. One British administrator in India in the 19th century flatly described Pathan attitudes as "tainted with rebellion and thoroughly obnoxious". Even the feudal rulers of

Afghanistan, themselves Pathans, have viewed their fellow-tribesmen with distaste and, sometimes, despair. When King Muhammad Yaqub was threatened with a Pathan rebellion during a war with the British in 1879, he declared in disgusted rage: "I would rather be a grass-cutter in the English camp than ruler of Afghanistan."

But, for all its murders, Pathan society is not lawless; nor is it unstable, despite the lack of formal criminal and civil law. An anarchic society could never have survived so long, outliving the empires that tried to crush it. The secret of Pathan resilience lies in the code of *pukhtunwali*, which imposes duties as well as gives rights; and in the *jirga*, the institution by which the community judges, then tries to resolve, private quarrels.

That Friday evening, Shams-ud Din tried to explain its workings. "Suppose there is a dispute between two men, who want to avoid bloodshed," he said. "The men might ask the village elders to form a *jirga* to settle the dispute. If the dispute involved families in addition to those of the two men, the elders might initiate the *jirga* themselves. We would gather in council to judge the rights and wrongs of the case, and we would try to find a compromise that would end the disagreement with justice for all."

The members of the *jirga* are elders of senior-lineage families whose social standing, experience and sagacity entitles them to a place on the council. Any Pathan who rejects their collective wisdom takes a grave risk, for a *jirga* can impose powerful sanctions to back up its judgment. It can put a man outside society, so that he is ignored by everyone in the village. It can confiscate his rifle or impose a heavy fine, payable to the other party in the dispute. If the man remains recalcitrant, the *jirga* can use force to bring him to book: sending men to burn down his house or, as a last resort, to shoot him dead.

As an example of a *jirga* case, Shams-ud Din cited a dispute he himself had recently had with one of his cousins, Innayat Khan, over the ownership of a field on the edges of Kado. Some years before, Shams-ud Din had spent much of his time farming an additional piece of land he owned in the settled area around the village of Bela Mohmandan, located just outside the tribal territories only a mile or two from Kado. In his absences, he had allowed this field at Kado to be sown and harvested by his cousin. Later, he asked his cousin to quit it so that his son Farmanullah could take over. Innayat refused. He argued that, having had its use and benefit for so long, it had become his property. It was the kind of dispute, Shams-ud Din said, that could have obliged him to retrieve the field by force. Instead, the cousin agreed to let the elders of Kado call a *jirga*. Then, instead of joining them in council, Shams-ud Din presented himself before them to argue his case. The *jirga*'s ruling was that the two men should divide the field and take half each, a compromise that pleased neither; but it did settle the dispute. Although Shams-ud Din's face darkened in anger when he spoke of what he still regarded as his cousin's treachery, there was no doubt that he had accepted the *jirga*'s verdict.

Jirgas can be called for many other reasons besides stopping a dispute before it has gone too far. Sometimes they are held after killings have taken place, to establish the facts of the case and to punish those who have not followed *pukhtunwali*. "Suppose a wife has an affair with her cousin," I was told, "and the husband, hearing of it, shoots both his wife and the cousin. Only then does the case go to the *jirga*." The mitigating circumstances of the killings will be discussed and, if the elders think the husband acted in haste, they may insist that he compensate the cousin's family with money or land. A man accused of kidnapping or stealing must also clear himself before a *jirga*.

Jirgas can be called also in cases involving whole communities rather than individuals. "We might hold a *jirga* to put a stop to clan warfare, or to discuss local matters, such as the possible sites for a new mosque or the financing of an irrigation project. We might even assemble to plan ways of persuading the government to increase the help it gives towards our sugar production."

The relations of the Pathans with the outside world have been conducted through *jirgas* ever since the 19th century, when the British had sought ways of dealing with the troublesome fighters on their North-West Frontier. In other parts of their empire, the British had usually managed to establish their rule through compliant local chiefs and kings and so at first they attempted to do the same among the Pathans. They offered privileges and money allowances to *maliks* they themselves had appointed. Such official *maliks*, however, were resented by the Pathans, who refused to co-operate with any formally established hierarchy. So the British compromised. They recognized the Pathans' traditional *jirgas* and offered written treaties guaranteeing non-interference in tribal affairs so long as the *jirgas* in their turn recognized the suzerainty of the British Raj.

Pakistan still honours these treaties and has made similar ones of its own. Sometimes, a *jirga* of tribal Pathans will assemble in the settled area to discuss local issues with the political agent or his deputy; on other occasions, the agent goes to the mountains and calls for a *jirga* within tribal territory. One celebrated government *jirga* was held in 1977, when fighting had broken

A Kado patriarch (centre) addresses his fellow elders, who have gathered in solemn council to adjudicate disputes among villagers. Council members are chosen by virtue of their age and shrewdness, and their accumulated prestige enables them to settle many conflicts without the violence endemic to Pathan disagreements.

out between two rival clans in the Orakzai Agency, a Pathan tribal area some 70 miles to the south of Mohmand territory. The clash was provoked by the long-disputed ownership of a three-acre field. Despite its petty origins, the confrontation soon escalated into a real shooting war. After skirmishes had cost three deaths and more than a dozen wounded, the well-armed rival groups dug in opposite each other along the 10-mile border between the clans. Everyday activity was paralyzed in an area of almost 80 square miles and clans related to the disputants threatened to become involved.

The political agent for the area then was the same Dr. Ahmed who had arranged for me to stay in Kado as Shams-ud Din's guest. Lacking the troops or the authority to enforce a peace, Dr. Ahmed acted with cunning. First, he obtained a cease-fire by means of *jirgas* held with the two sides separately; respect for the government helped to ensure at least temporary compliance. Next, he assembled between 50 and 60 respected tribal elders from all over the Orakzai Agency and asked them to act as a *jirga* to settle the dispute once and for all. The social standing of the *jirga* members made it difficult for the combatants not to accept their judgment. Dr. Ahmed had also taken into account the combatants' obligation to provide hospitality for the *jirga*. To avoid offending the dignity of the elders, cattle and sheep had to be slaughtered and cooked twice daily, then served with the best quality rice and bread. The cost of feeding so many guests in the manner required by *pukhtunwali* was crippling for their hosts. The expense of such lavish hospitality, on top of the cost of the fighting itself, probably had much to do with the fact that an acceptable peace was agreed upon within a few days.

The crisis ended with a grand tribal assembly organized by Dr. Ahmed. As a suitable place for the reconciliation of the two sides, he had chosen a ridge where some famous battles had been fought against the British in 1897, a location calculated to remind the tribesmen of their essential unity. "Elders met, laughed and joked across the dining table for the first time since the shooting began," he wrote in a later account of the affair. "Seeing them, I was made aware of the intimacy and warmth of kinship that was divided by a thin line from hatred and bitterness."

At 7 a.m. on the morning appointed for the Kado *jirga*, the elders gathered under the shade of a large open-sided shelter in Nur Rahman's *hujra*. They were to hear the case of Selim versus Haji Gul. Selim, Haji Gul's father, had asked for the *jirga* to assemble, claiming that his son refused to support him financially in his old age. Selim had a few rocky acres of his own, but his son had brought back a tidy sum from a stint in the oilfields of Saudi Arabia and the old man, who had no love for labour on the land, felt entitled to a share. While in Saudi Arabia, Haji Gul had taken time off for a pilgrimage to Mecca: "Haji", meaning pilgrim, is a title that may be awarded to Muslims who accomplish the journey. Secure in the status that his religious devotion had brought him, the young man was determined to resist his father's demands.

As we made our way towards the *hujra*, Shams-ud Din explained to me that only the elders and those directly involved in the case would be allowed to speak, but many of the younger men would sit behind them and listen to what was going on. In this way, the customs of the tribe were passed down from generation to generation.

The older men sat down in a semicircle on the ground and discussed the case informally until Selim, a stooped and elderly man, arrived. Holding out their hands in a position of supplication, they called out: "May God give us strength to be just." Passing their hands down over their faces and beards, they requested Selim to sit in front of them while he put his case.

"Shams-ud Din," Nur Rahman began, turning to address his respected colleague. "You ask him why he spends all his time disputing with his son, and then comes complaining to us." Shams-ud Din did so and Selim presented his position—that it should be a matter of honour for a man to support an aging father and that, since his own son was well known to be wealthy as a result of his labour abroad, it was only just that he should give at least 2,000 rupees. Selim needed the money, he claimed, to keep himself in what he considered to be decent comfort. It was clear from the expressions on the elders' faces that they had little sympathy for Selim and did not regard him as a man who had been greatly wronged. The reason, it transpired, was that Selim had a well-deserved reputation as the most cantankerous old pest in the village.

Having heard his case, they sent Selim away and called the son. Haji Gul seemed to have come to the *jirga* reluctantly and wore an air of belligerence. Still, he listened politely as Shams-ud Din put his father's case to him.

"Why are you refusing to give your father 2,000 rupees?"

"I have no bad conscience about this," replied Haji Gul. "I discharge my duty. But my father is a greedy man and has always been a nuisance. He continually demands more money from me and I keep on giving it to him."

The elders reacted to these comments with some amusement and conferred among themselves for a few minutes. Turning back to Haji Gul, they warned him that, when they had made a decision, they expected him to abide by it. Haji Gul grudgingly agreed that he would accept their findings, but added that they must make sure that his father would not ask for more later. Again the elders conferred. Then Shams-ud Din told Haji Gul: "You must accept that, if either of you ignores our decision, we will impose a fine of 10,000 rupees." Having warned of the cost of defying their authority—10,000 rupees was more than a year's income for the average villager—the elders sent Haji Gul away and began to discuss what should be done.

Age is respected very highly by Pathans and all the men passing judgment at this *jirga* were greybeards—most of them in their sixties. Although they recognized that Selim was a difficult man, it was natural that they should feel some sympathy for one of their contemporaries. Even Nur Rahman, at 50 one of the youngest of the decision-makers, was keen to provide some form of compromise. "Yes, we know Selim is a corrupt, bitter man. But he is still Haji Gul's father and as a greybeard he should be treated gently. Because he is old and cannot do much work, something should be given to him."

"But Haji Gul was right," Shams-ud Din pointed out. "I know that Selim kept pestering Haji Gul's wife for rupees while her husband was away earning

Outside the mud-brick structures of Kado village, the tribal council assembles to oversee the drawing of a line that will divide a field between two

cousins, both of whom claimed the whole. Such disputes can be violent, but on this occasion the council's compromise produced a peaceful solution.

158

money in Arabia. Perhaps if we show our concern about his grasping habits, he will not keep bothering his son."

The old men argued and discussed the case for the better part of an hour. Behind them, the younger men were making their own observations, but the elders—when they overheard—turned and sharply rebuked them for interfering. Eventually the *jirga* came to a decision. Normally one of the senior elders would have given the verdict, but on this occasion a holy man, Mian Zarif, happened to be visiting the village. For reasons that were later made clear to me, the assembly decided to ask Mian Zarif to deliver the verdict. Shams-ud Din ordered a chair to be brought as a mark of honour and one of the young men was despatched to fetch Mian Zarif. A portly, bearded man dressed in white robes, wearing a large white turban round a blue cap, he appeared through the trees at the edge of the *hujra* and was ushered with great respect to the chair. Sitting down, he nodded sagely as Shams-ud Din explained the details of the case and the decision that had been reached.

Haji Gul and Selim were summoned before the elders again. "The tribe has called a *jirga* to settle your dispute," Mian Zarif told them in a loud voice. "The *jirga*'s decision is a just one and follows Islamic principles. Haji Gul, you will pay your father 1,000 rupees; and you, Selim, will accept the 1,000 rupees and not demand more. The *jirga* will not listen to another demand and will impose a fine of 10,000 rupees if either of you refuses to accept these findings. You must now embrace and accept the decision. And you, Haji Gul, must kiss your father on his beard."

Mian Zarif placed one large hand on Selim's shoulder and the other on his son's shoulder, then propelled the two men together. Everyone burst out laughing as an obviously reluctant Haji Gul clasped his father and stooped to kiss his beard. Having achieved this stage-managed reconciliation, Mian Zarif said a brief prayer and the *jirga* was over.

Mian Zarif now allowed himself a small jibe at the customs of the Pathans. "Tell your English friend," he told Ihsanullah good-humouredly, "that because the Mohmands always want to fight each other, they need wise men like me to help them keep the peace."

Later, I discussed with Ihsanullah the part played by Mian Zarif. "Has he any connection with Kado?" I asked. "No," Ihsanullah replied. "He is not even a Pathan, but we trust him because he has knowledge and is a man of God." Mian was not his name, Ihsanullah added, but his title. The *mians*, a religious order similar to the *pirs*, or pious men, are believed to be descended from the Prophet Muhammad's own tribe. In spite of his high religious status, however, Mian Zarif could not have joined in the discussions of the *jirga*: only Pathans may take part in that.

Their religious status, coupled with their lack of kin ties to any Pathan tribe, combine to make it especially appropriate for the *mians* to act as peacemakers in feuds and disputes. In the days before the government had any involvement in tribal affairs their intervention was often the only means of reconciling belligerents. Unaffected by the laws of revenge, they can travel without arms and without fear throughout the tribal areas. On occasion they

A boy pores over his arithmetic homework in a corner of a Kado compound. The village school, set up by the Pakistan Government in the late 1970s, also teaches the Koran, geography and the Pathan tribal language. Education is free, but attendance is poor; girls do not attend school at all and a typical youth quits after just two years.

have been able to obtain a cease-fire simply by carrying a white flag and walking between warring groups, then talking them into calling a *jirga*.

It occurred to me, after watching the *jirga* in action in Kado, that such proceedings served as more than the high court of *pukhtunwali*; they were also a kind of university for Pathan values and behaviour. The discussions held by the village elders were a highly effective way to teach young Pathan men the real meaning of *pukhtunwali*. "When I was a boy," Ihsanullah told me, "my father and grandfather spent a lot of time trying to explain to me what the code of honour meant. But it was only when I saw my elders in council at a *jirga* that I really understood."

Ihsanullah believed strongly in perpetuating the traditions of the tribe. Having graduated, through attendance at *jirgas*, to a secondary level of initiation into *pukhtunwali*, Ihsanullah in his turn often spent time passing on his knowledge to the village children, at the primary level.

Ihsanullah was by Pathan standards a well-educated man, and he was also keen to teach what he had learnt from the outside world. He was willing to do so in ways that would have shocked his ancestors; on one occasion, I saw him giving a reading lesson to a group of girls. Until the coming of Pakistan's independence in 1947, education—even for boys—had been regarded as unmanly; any Mohmands who went to school in British India were taunted for their softness, but education for girls was regarded as downright improper. The Mohmands grudgingly accepted limited schooling for their girls in the late 1950s; but as recently as 1977, when the first two girls' primary schools were opened in the Orakzai area, the women teachers who had been brought from Peshawar were threatened with abduction by hostile tribesmen and had to be protected by an armed escort.

Yet, I could now see Ihsanullah happily teaching these girls in a male bastion: a *hujra* that had been temporarily deserted by its habitués. With their backs against a mud wall, the girls sat clutching at tattered exercise books or scraps of paper. There were about 10 of them, ranging in age from three to 11 or 12. The older girls were already conscious of the approach of *purdah* and, when they became aware that I was watching them, demurely pulled their veils over their faces. The younger ones just giggled and looked down at their feet, poking out of their baggy trousers.

Ihsanullah called on them, one by one, to bring their books, sit in front of him and recite the letters of the Arabic alphabet. "*Alef*," he called out to a pretty girl sitting cross-legged in front of him; "*Aa-alef*," the girl repeated timidly. "*Jimah!*" "*Jimah*," she whispered back. And so it continued.

When the lesson had finished, I asked Ihsanullah just what he had been teaching and to what end. "It is their mothers who teach them to be good honourable Pathan women and who prepare them for their future as wives," he said. "I teach them how to read and how to understand the Koran. They cannot be good wives unless they are good Muslims, and for that they need to be able to pray properly and to read a little."

After sending the girls away, Ihsanullah lined up a group of boys he had collected from all over the village. His teaching now took on a different purpose.

A youth steels himself against the recoil of his rifle during a lesson in marksmanship. As befits a volatile people, Pathans place high value on skill with arms. The boy's teacher carries impressive credentials: he fled from his own village, with honour, after killing a neighbour in a dispute concerning rights to irrigation water.

"A boy can learn to read and write in school," he explained. "What I try to teach them is how to behave as good Muslim Mohmands." Each boy had covered his head with a cap or a cloth. Under the watchful eye of Ihsanullah they performed praying exercises. When a boy did not properly have his head bowed or his forehead touching the ground, or if he had forgotten the words of a prayer, Ihsanullah rebuked him while the others giggled complacently.

Predictably, Ihsanullah considered the lessons he gave the boys to be far more vital than those for the girls. "But most important of all," he explained, "is what the boys learn from their fathers and grandfathers. They have to know how to fight—and why to fight. We could forgive you, as an outsider and a guest, for making mistakes and causing insult. But we would never forgive one of us for doing the same. A boy has to know when he might be making a mistake or when someone else might be insulting him."

To keep up his position in the tribe and to follow the strict rules of revenge laid down by the code of *pukhtunwali*, a boy had to acquire fighting ability; his whole status as a Pathan depended on it. A boy is thought to become a man at 10 or 12, but the Pathans insist that a boy is never too young to avenge an insult to his family. Education in the martial arts was daily in progress around me. Ten-year-olds played with slingshots, expertly knocking down improvised targets or felling birds from trees. When it came to rifle shooting, the men of the village were enthusiastic teachers, and all of the boys appeared to be proficient in the use of their fathers' weapons. Furthermore, any 12-year-old boy was already accustomed by that age to accompanying his grandfather as an armed escort on journeys, both to ensure the elder's safety and to emphasize the old man's status.

Before coming to Mohmand territory I had read Winston Churchill's account of the people and the area, written in the 1890s when he was a young officer on campaign in the North-West Frontier Province. I had thought that his account would provide interesting historical background. "Amid these scenes of savage brilliancy," the future British leader wrote, "there dwells a race whose qualities seem to harmonize with their environment. Except at harvest time, when self-preservation enjoins a temporary truce, the Pathan tribes are always engaged in private or public war. Every man is a warrior, a politician and a theologian. Every village has its defence. Every family cultivates its vendetta; every clan, its feud. The numerous tribes and combinations of tribes all have their accounts to settle with one another. Nothing is ever forgotten, and very few debts are left unpaid. For the purposes of social life, a most elaborate code of honour has been established and is on the whole faithfully observed. A man who knew it and observed it faultlessly might pass unharmed from one end of the frontier to another. The slightest technical slip would, however, be fatal." At the end of my own visit to the tribal territories I tried to assess whether Churchill's character sketch of the Pathans was still valid.

Since he wrote that assessment, of course, many changes have taken place. In 1975, a good tarmac road was driven through the centre of the tribal area;

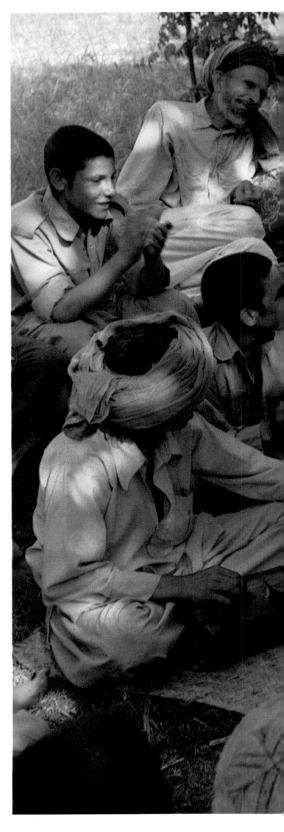

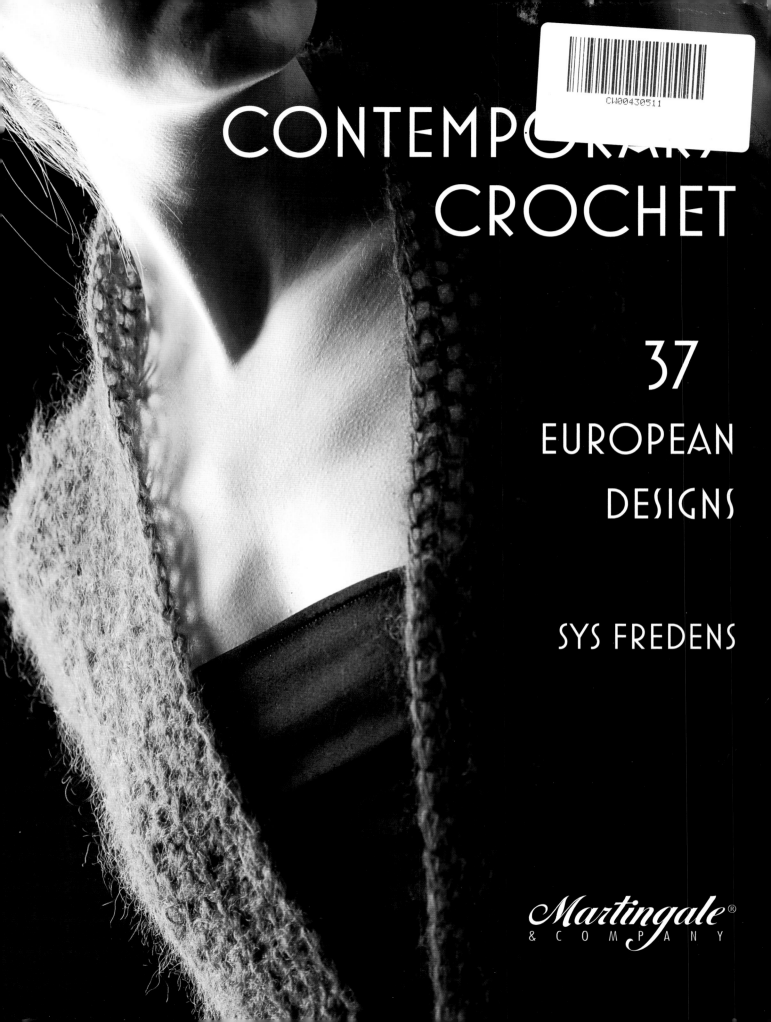

CONTEMPORARY CROCHET

37 EUROPEAN DESIGNS

SYS FREDENS

Martingale®
& COMPANY

Contemporary Crochet: 37 European Designs
© 2009 by Sys Fredens

Martingale & Company
20205 144th Ave. NE
Woodinville, WA 98072-8478 USA
www.martingale-pub.com

Printed in China
13 12 11 10 09 08   8 7 6 5 4 3 2 1

Library of Congress Cataloging-in-Publication Data
is available upon request.

ISBN: 978-1-56477-897-0

The original Danish editions were published as *Hæklerier* and *Nye hæklerier*.

Hæklerier
Copyright text © Sys Fredens
Copyright photos © Sys Fredens & Morten Keblovszki
Copyright © 2006 Forlaget Klematis A/S, Denmark (www.klematis.dk)

Nye hæklerier
Copyright text © Sys Fredens
Copyright photos © Jakob Lerche
Copyright © 2006 Forlaget Klematis A/S, Denmark (www.klematis.dk)

This edition is published by arrangement with Claudia Böhme Rights & Literary Agency, Hannover, Germany (www.agency-boehme.com).

Mission Statement
Dedicated to providing quality products and service to inspire creativity.

Credits
President & CEO: Tom Wierzbicki

Editorial Director: Mary V. Green

Managing Editor: Tina Cook

Translator: Carol Huebscher Rhoades

Technical Editor: Ursula Reikes

Supplementary Pattern Sizing: Susan Huxley

Copy Editor: Liz McGehee

Design Director: Stan Green

Production Manager: Regina Girard

Illustrator: Laurel Strand

Cover Designer: Stan Green

Text Designer: Regina Girard

CONTENTS

PROJECT GALLERY

Triangular
Shawl 12

Shell-Pattern
Shawl 14

Fringed
Fleece
Shawl 16

Jaunty
Tam 18

Hat with
Brim 20

Matching Cap, Scarf, and Mittens 22

Sun Hat
26

Summer
Bag
28

Net Shopping Bag   30

Flowers and
Leaves   32

Summer Top   34

V-Neck Top   36

A-Line Skirt
38

Kid Mohair Vest   40

Three-Tier Skirt   42

Summer Top with Shoulder Bands   44

Wraparound Skirt   46

Halter Top   48

Fishnet
Stockings
50

Sleeveless
Top 52

Mohair Top, with or without Sleeves 54

Wide-Neck
Top 56

Two-Color
Mohair
Sweater
58

V-Neck Sweater 60

Button-Collar
Sweater 62

Deep V-Neck
Sweater
with Collar
65

Wraparound Sweater 68

Sweater with Wide Collar 70

Side-to-Side Sweater 72

Hooded Jacket 75

V-Neck
Dress 78

Hooded
Cape 80

Shawl-Collared Jacket 82

Tunisian Jacket 84

Coat with
Shawl Collar 88

INTRODUCTION

Crocheters, if you're ready to take your wardrobe in a new direction for more sophistication and style, the fashion adventure begins here! Martingale & Company is proud to bring you the latest in crocheted clothing and accessories by Danish designer Sys Fredens. Now you can look as if you've just returned from Europe—without leaving your favorite chair!

Just browse through these stunning photos and you'll find plenty to inspire you. The first few pages feature lovely shawls to fling about your shoulders or bestow as impressive gifts, followed by an assortment of irresistible hats, including a jaunty tam and a romantic sun hat.

You'll also find contemporary bags for carrying your things and showing off your artistry. Maybe you'd like a net bag for shopping or an oversized bag for a day at the beach. Throw one over your shoulder and strike a pose in any of the sassy sleeveless summer tops—and don't miss the eye-catching halter top.

The wide assortment of designs includes something for every season, so you'll always have just the thing to wear. Choose from flirty, feminine skirts and cozy, comfortable sweaters. Try a hooded cape or a V-neck dress. Or step out in daring fashion in a pair of fishnet stockings!

As you begin, you'll discover that each project is as fun to make as it is to wear. Simple-to-follow instructions and clear illustrations allow you to relax and enjoy the creative process. These garments and accessories were crocheted with yarn available in Europe, but we've made it easy to find beautiful yarn that's similar, close to home. Rather than limiting you to a specific fiber and manufacturer, each project lists the type of yarn to use. Simply refer to the "Standard Yarn-Weight System" on page 94, and you'll find the perfect materials for every piece.

So pack some luxurious yarn and a simple hook and take a vacation in your favorite chair. Soon you'll be strolling through town in a smartly styled "souvenir" from Europe. This book is the ticket!

TRIANGULAR SHAWL

*You can't have too many shawls. There are many
ways to wrap a shawl, or you can secure it
with a brooch. Shawls crocheted with mohair,
like this one, weigh almost nothing.*

Finished Measurements

Approx 25½" x 67"

Materials

100 g; 196 yds of bulky-weight mohair **5**

12 mm crochet hook

Gauge

4 sts and 3 rows = 4" in dc

Instructions

The shawl starts at the lower edge and is shaped with inc at the center.

At end of all rows, turn and ch 3 (counts as 1 dc).

Ch 3 and work 3 dc in 3rd ch from hook = 4 dc.

Row 1: Work 2 dc in base of turning ch, (2 dc in next st) twice, 1 dc in turning ch = 8 dc.

Row 2: Work 1 dc in base of turning ch, 2 dc in next st, 1 dc in each of next 2 sts, 2 dc in next st, 1 dc, 1 dc in turning ch = 10 dc.

Row 3: Work 1 dc in base of turning ch and in each st across, 2 dc in turning chain = 12 dc.

Row 4: Work 1 dc in first st, 4 dc, (2 dc in next st) twice, 4 dc, 2 dc in turning chain = 16 dc.

Row 5: Work 1 dc in base of turning ch and in each st across, 2 dc in turning chain = 18 dc.

Row 6: Work 1 dc in base of turning ch, 7 dc, (2 dc in next st) twice, 7 dc, 2 dc in turning chain = 22 dc.

Rep rows 5 and 6, working increasingly more dc before and after the center inc and always working inc over the previous ones at center of shawl. Cont until yarn runs out.

Weave in ends.

SHELL-PATTERN SHAWL

This shawl is worked in a shell pattern—a classic combination of double crochet and chain stitches. The thick alpaca yarn makes an especially cozy shawl for cool evenings.

Finished Measurements

Approx 24" x 55"

Materials

300 g; 656 yds of bulky-weight alpaca **5**

8 mm crochet hook

Gauge

1 shell = 2¼" wide and 1" high

Shell Pattern

Ch 3.

Row 1: Into 3rd ch from hook, work 2 dc, ch 1, 2 dc = 1 shell. Turn with ch 4.

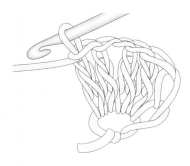

Row 2: Work 1 dc in base of turning chain. (At center of shell on previous row, work 2 dc, ch 1, 2 dc), 1 dc in turning loop. Turn and ch 4.

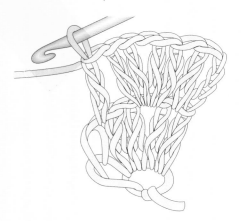

Row 3: Work 1 dc in base of turning ch. (At center of shell on previous row, work 2 dc, ch 1, 2 dc); in turning loop, work 2 dc, ch 1, 2 dc. Turn and ch 4.

Rep row 3 throughout.

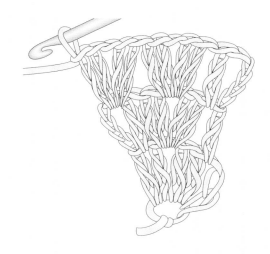

Instructions

At end of all rows, turn and ch 4.

Ch 3.

Row 1: Work (2 dc, ch 1, 2 dc) in 3rd ch from hook (1 shell made).

Row 2: Work 1 dc in base of turning ch, (2 dc, ch 1, 2 dc) in ch-1 sp of next shell on previous row, 1 dc in turning loop = 1 shell.

Row 3: Work 1 dc in base of turning ch, *(2 dc, ch 1, 2 dc) in ch-1 sp of next shell on previous row, rep from * across to last dc, work (2 dc, ch 1, 2 dc) between last dc and turning ch = 2 shells.

Rep row 3 until there are 25 shells across. Turn and ch 1.

Work a row of sl sts along long edge.

Weave in ends.

FRINGED
FLEECE SHAWL

*This warm fleece shawl,
with its wide crocheted edgings
and fringe, makes a great gift.*

Finished Measurements

Approx 19½" x 63" (excluding fringe)

Materials

50 g; 164 yds of light worsted–weight mohair/wool blend (3)

Piece of fleece, approx 20" x 63"

2.5 mm and 4 mm crochet hooks

Large, sharp-pointed tapestry needle

Instructions

Trim the rough selvage from the fleece, but *do not* cut away the small holes along the selvage. You will work the edging into these holes.

Single-crochet edge: With smaller hook, work 1 sc in each of the small holes along the cut edge. You should have approx 15 sts per 4" or a total of 75 sts. Turn work. Use the tapestry needle to widen holes.

Chain-stitch loops: Change to larger hook, *ch 3, sk 2 sc, work 1 sc in next st; rep from * across row = 25 loops. Turn and ch 2.

Shells: Work (1 tr, ch 1, 1 tr, 1 dc) in first loop, ch 1, *work (1 dc, 1 tr, ch 1, 1 tr, 1 dc) in next loop, ch 1; rep from * across. Turn and ch 4.

Chain-stitch loops: *Work 1 sc in ch-1 sp at center of next shell, ch 4, work 1 sc in ch-1 sp between shells, ch 4; rep from * across, end with 1 sc in ch-1 sp at center of last shell, ch 4, work 1 sl st in last dc.

Rep the edging on the opposite end of the fleece.

Fringe: Cut 208 strands of yarn, 12" long. Using 4 strands for each fringe, knot fringe into every other ch sp on both ends.

Weave in ends.

JAUNTY TAM

*This smart and warm tam starts with a
band long enough to go around your head.
Then the crown is worked in single crochet
with a larger crochet hook.*

Finished Measurement

Circumference: Approx 21¼"

Materials

100 g; 142 yds of worsted-weight yarn (4)

5 mm and 12 mm crochet hooks

Gauge

8 sts and 6 rows = 4" in sc on larger hook

Instructions

Band: With smaller hook, ch 6. Sc in 2nd ch from hook and in each sc across = 5 sc. Turn and ch 1.

Work in sc until 60 rows are completed and piece measures approx 21¼" long. Join short ends of band with sl st, and ch 1.

Crown: Work (1 sc, ch 2) in every other row around the band = 30 ch loops.

Change to larger hook and work as follows, joining rnds with sl st and ch 1: *Work 1 sc in first loop, 2 sc in next loop*, rep from * to * around = 45 sts.

Crochet without further shaping until piece measures 6" from band.

Top shaping: Work (1 sc, sc2tog) around. Rep this dec rnd 2 more times.

Cut yarn and use tail to tighten hole at center of crown.

Weave in ends.

HAT WITH BRIM

Put the finishing touch on your outfit with this stylish hat. It's crocheted with a brim that folds up at the back.

Finished Measurement

Circumference: Approx 21½"

Materials

200 g; 153 yds of bulky-weight wool 🔳**5**

8 mm crochet hook

Gauge

8 sts and 9 rows = 4" in sc

Instructions

End each rnd with sl st in first st of rnd, then ch 1 unless otherwise indicated.

Ch 4 and join into a ring with sl st. Ch 1.

Rnd 1: Work 2 sc in each st = 8 sts.

Rnd 2: Work 2 sc in each st = 16 sts.

Rnd 3: *Work 2 sc in next st, 1 sc in next st; rep from * around = 24 sts.

Rnd 4: *Work 2 sc in next st, 1 sc in each of next 2 sts; rep from * around = 32 sts.

Rnd 5: *Work 2 sc in next st, 1 sc in each of next 3 sts; rep from * around = 40 sts.

Pm in 20th and 40th sts to indicate center front and center back.

Rnd 6: *Work 1 sc in each of next 19 sts, 2 sc in next st (marked st); rep from * once = 42 sts.

Rnd 7: Sc around.

Rnd 8: *Work 1 sc in each of next 20 sc, 2 sc in next st; rep from * once = 44 sts.

Cont rnds in sc without further shaping until piece is about 6" from rnd 8.

Brim

Next rnd: Work 1 sc in each of next 12 sc, 2 sc in next st, 5 sc, 2 sc in next st, 6 sc, 2 sc in next st, 5 sc, 2 sc in next st (4-st inc), 1 sl st in next st = 48 sts. Turn and ch 1.

Next rnd: Sl st in first st, sc in each of next 24 sts, sl st in next st. Turn and ch 1.

Next rnd: Sl st in first st, sc to end of rnd.

Next rnd: Sc around.

Next rnd: Work 8 sc, 2 sc in next st, (5 sc, 2 sc in next st) twice, 6 sc, 2 sc in next st, (5 sc, 2 sc in next st) twice (6-st inc), sl st in next st. Turn and ch 1.

Next rnd: Sl st in next st, sc in each of next 38 sts, sl st in next st. Turn and ch 1.

Next rnd: Sl st in first st, sc to end of rnd.

Next 2 rnds: Sc around.

Weave in ends.

MATCHING CAP, SCARF, AND MITTENS

This colorful, cozy set works up quickly in bulky-weight wool. Working double crochet through only the back loops creates the ridges in the pattern on the cap and mittens.

CAP

Finished Measurement

Circumference: Approx 20½"

Materials

150 g; 98 yds of multicolored, bulky-weight merino wool (5)

9 mm crochet hook

Gauge

8 sts and 8 rows = 4" in sc through back loops

Instructions

Work sc in back loops only. This makes ridges on the right side.

Join every rnd with sl st in first st, then ch 1.

Ch 40 and join into a ring with sl st, ch 1. Mark beg of rnd with a contrast yarn and move it up on each rnd.

Sc around until piece measures 4¾" from beg ring.

Crown Shaping

Rnd 1: *Sc2tog, work 1 sc in each of next 3 sc; rep from * around = 32 sts.

Rnds 2 and 4: Sc around.

Rnd 3: *Sc2tog, work 1 sc in each of next 2 sc; rep from * around = 24 sts.

Rnd 5: *Sc2tog, work 1 sc in next st; rep from * around = 16 sts.

Rnd 6: Sc around.

Rnd 7: (Sc2tog, work 1 sc in next st) 4 times, sc2tog twice = 6 sts.

Sc around these 6 sts for 1½".

Cut yarn, bring tail through last st.

Weave in ends.

SCARF

Finished Measurements

Approx 9½" x 59"

Materials

350 g; 230 yds of multicolored, bulky-weight merino wool (5)

15 mm crochet hook

Gauge

5 sts and 6 rows = 4" in dc

Instructions

At end of all rows, turn and ch 3 (counts as 1 dc).

Ch 14. Dc in 3rd ch from hook and in each dc across = 12 dc.

Work 1 dc in next st and in each dc across, work last dc in top of turning ch = 12 dc.

Cont in dc until scarf measures 59" long.

Cut yarn, pull through last st.

Weave in ends.

MITTENS

Finished Measurements

Hand circumference: Approx 9"

Length: Approx 12½"

Materials

200 g; 130 yds of multicolored, bulky-weight merino wool 〔**5**〕

9 mm crochet hook

Gauge

8 sts and 8 rows = 4" in sc through back loops

Instructions

Work sc in back loops only. This makes ridges on the right side.

Join every rnd with sl st in the first st, then ch 1.

Ch 18 and join into a ring with 1 sl st, ch 1. Mark beg of rnd with a contrast yarn and move it up on each rnd.

Next rnd: Sc around.

Rep last rnd until mitten measures 4¾" from beg.

Thumb Gusset

Rnd 1 (inc rnd): Work 1 sc in next 12 sc, 2 sc in each of next 2 sc, 1 sc in next 4 sc = 20 sc.

Rnds 2 and 4: Sc around.

Rnd 3: Work 1 sc in next 13 sc, 2 sc in each of next 2 sc, 1 sc in next 5 sc = 22 sc.

Rnd 5: Work 1 sc in next 14 sc, 2 sc in each of next 2 sc, 1 sc in next 6 sc = 24 sc.

Rnd 6: Work 1 sc in next 13 sc, ch 2, sk 6 sc, sc in next 5 sc = 18 sc. You now have a hole for the thumb.

Work in sc on 18 sts until mitten measures 10½" from beg.

Mitten Top

Rnd 1: Work (1 sc in next 2 sc, sc2tog) 4 times, 1 sc in next 2 sc = 14 sc.

Rnd 2: Work (1 sc in next 2 sc, sc2tog) 3 times, 1 sc in next 2 sc = 11 sc.

Rnd 3: Work 1 sc in next 2 sc, (sc2tog, 1 sc in next sc) 3 times = 8 sc.

Cut yarn and sew top of mitten tog.

Thumb

Work 10 sc around thumbhole and cont around for 1½".

Shape thumb top:

Rnd 1: Work (1 sc, sc2tog) 3 times, 1 sc in last sc = 7 sc.

Rnd 2: Work (1 sc, sc2tog) twice, 1 sc in last sc = 5 sc.

Cut yarn and sew top of thumb tog.

Make other mitten the same way, but place thumbhole on opposite side of palm.

Weave in ends.

*A romantic hat provides lovely
protection on a sunny day.*

Finished Measurement

Circumference: Small: Approx 19¾
(Medium: Approx 21¼)"

Materials

100 (150) g; 306 (460) yds of light worsted–weight linen/polyester blend **3**

3 mm crochet hook

2 pieces of organza ribbon, ¼" wide and 39½" long, in different colors

Removable stitch marker

Gauge

4 shells and 12 rows = 4"

Instructions

Mark beg of rnd with removable marker and move up each rnd.

Crown

Ch 6 (8) and join into a ring with sl st, ch 1.

Rnd 1: Work 10 (16) sc into ring. Join every rnd with sl st and ch 2 (does not count as st).

Rnd 2: Work 2 dc in each sc around = 20 (32) sts.

Rnd 3: Work (1 dc, 2 dc in next st) around = 30 (48 sts).

Rnd 4: Work 2 dc in every (every other) st around = 60 (72 sts).

Rnd 5: (The ch 2 after joining now counts for 1 dc; work 3 dc into first st) = 1 shell, (sk 2 sts, work 4 dc in next st) around = 20 (24) shells.

Rep rnd 5 until there are a total of 15 (16) rounds of shells.

Brim

Work 1 rnd in sc (except on size Small, sk 1 st at beg and center of rnd) = 78 (96) sts. Join every rnd with sl st and ch 2.

Rnds 1, 2, 3, and 4: (The ch 2 counts as 1 dc; work 3 dc in first st) = 1 shell; (sk 2 sts, work 4 dc in next st) around = 26 (32) shells.

Rnd 5: Work as for rnd 1, but ch 1 between each shell.

Rnd 6: Work as for rnd 1 with the following change: work 4 dc in first st, and 5 dc for all rem shells.

Weave in ends.

Wind silk ribbons around hat above brim and tie into a bow.

SUMMER BAG

*Carry your things in style with
this generously sized bag.*

Finished Measurements

Circumference: Approx 25½" at widest point

Length (excluding handles): Approx 12"

Materials

250 g; 380 yds of bulky-weight cotton/linen blend
[5]

5 mm crochet hook

Gauge

3.5 patt rep and 6 rows = 4"

Sides (Make 2)

With 1 strand of yarn, ch 36.

Row 1: Sc in 3rd ch from hook, (ch 2, sk 2 sts, work 1 sc) across. Turn and ch 2.

Row 2: *Work (1 sc, ch 2, 3 dc) in next ch-2 sp; rep from * to beg ch-2, sc in sp = 11 patt. Turn and ch 4.

Row 3: *Work (1 sc, ch 2, 3 dc) in ch-2 sp; rep from * to beg ch-4, sc in sp. Turn and ch 4.

Rep row 3 until piece measures 12" long. Cut yarn.

Crochet the 2 pieces tog at sides with sc, leaving top 4" open.

Base

With 2 strands of yarn held tog, work 44 sc around bottom edge of bag.

Cont around in sc, work sc2tog at each side of side seams (4-st dec per rnd) = 40 sts.

Work 3 more dec rnds = 28 sts after 3rd dec rnd.

Cut yarn and sew base tog.

Handle

With 1 strand of yarn, ch 2, dc in first ch, *dc into st below hook, just to left of first strand of yarn, ch 1, rep from * until cord measures 31". Weave cord in and out of the holes 2 rows down from top edge,

skipping the center 4 patt on each side. Sew ends of cord tog to form a ring.

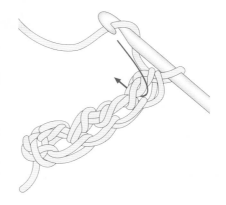

Weave in ends.

NET SHOPPING BAG

It's easy and fun to crochet a net bag for shopping or a day at the beach. Grab your hook and get going!

Finished Measurements

Circumference: Approx 24" at widest point

Length (excluding handles): Approx 14"

Materials

300 g; 136 yds of bulky-weight cotton ribbon, ½" wide **5**

9 mm crochet hook

Removable stitch marker

Gauge

6 sts and 3 rows = 4" in tr

Base

Ch 5 and join into a ring with sl st. Ch 1.

Rnd 1: Work 9 sc in ring, join with sl st in ch at beg of rnd. Ch 3.

Mark beg of rnd with a removable marker and move it up on each rnd.

End each rnd with sl st in top of turning ch and ch 3 (counts as 1 st).

Rnd 2: Work 1 dc in next sc, 2 dc in each sc around = 18 sts.

Bag

Rnd 3: *Work 2 tr in next st, 1 tr in next st; rep from * around = 27 sts.

Rnd 4: *Work 2 tr in next st, 1 tr in each of next 2 sts; rep from * around to last 2 sts, work 2 tr in next st, 1 tr in last st = 36 sts.

Work even in tr until bag measures 14" from rnd 1. End last rnd with sl st in top of turning ch and ch 1.

Edging

Work 2 rnds in sc.

Handles

Work 4 sl sts along edging and then 1 dc, *dc into st below hook, just to left of first strand of yarn, ch 1; rep from * until handle measures 19" long. See "Handle" on page 29.

Sk 7 sts and join handle to edging with sc. Sl st 9 and crochet other handle as for first. Sl st to end of rnd.

Weave in ends.

FLOWERS AND LEAVES

*Decorate a basket with an abundance of flowers,
or make one or two for a lapel or a hat.*

Materials

Flowers: 50 g; 150 yds of light worsted–weight cotton/rayon blend in each of the following colors: rose, old rose, rust, burgundy, yellow, light turquoise, and blue [3]

Leaves: 50 g; 180 yds of light worsted–weight cotton/metallic blend in green [3]

4 mm crochet hook for flowers

3 mm crochet hook for leaves

Decorative basket and fine-gauge wire for attaching flowers

Flower (Make 18)

At end of each row, turn and ch 3 (counts as 1 dc).

With 4 mm hook, ch 43.

Row 1: Dc in 4th ch from hook and in each ch across = 40 dc.

Row 2: Work 1 dc, (ch 1, 1 dc) across.

Row 3: Work 1 dc, (ch 1, 1 dc in ch-1 sp, ch 1, 1 dc in next st) across.

Row 4: Work 1 dc in ch-1 sp, (ch 3, 1 dc in next ch-1 sp) across.

Starting at one end, roll piece along row 1 and seam along beg ch-st row.

Make a total of 18 flowers: 3 rose, 3 old rose, 2 rust, 3 burgundy, 2 yellow, 2 light turquoise, and 3 blue.

Leaf (Make 18)

With smaller hook and green, ch 12.

Sc in 2nd ch from hook and in next 9 sc, work 3 sc in last sc, 10 sc along other side of beg ch = 23 sc. Do not turn.

Row 1: Work 3 sc in next st (stem), 9 sc; turn and ch 1.

Row 2: Work 10 sc, 3 sc in next st, 10 sc; turn and ch 1.

Row 3: Work 11 sc, 3 sc in next st, 9 sc; turn and ch 1.

Row 4: Work 10 sc, 3 sc in next st, 10 sc; turn and ch 1.

Row 5: Work 11 sc, 3 sc in next st, 9 sc; turn and ch 1.

Row 6: Work 10 sc, 3 sc in next st, 10 sc; turn and ch 1.

Row 7: Work 11 sc. Cut yarn.

Weave in ends.

Fasten the leaves and flowers to basket edge with wire.

SUMMER TOP

*Here's an easy design
with a square neckline.*

Finished Measurements

Bust: 31 (33, 35, 37)"

Length: 17¾ (18½, 19¾, 21¾)"

Materials

200 (200, 250, 300) g; 612 (612, 765, 930) yds of light worsted–weight linen and polyester yarn (**3**)

4 mm crochet hook

Gauge

15 sts and 19 rows = 4" in sc

Back

At end of all rows, turn and ch 1.

Ch 59 (63, 67, 71). Sc in 2nd ch from hook and in each ch across = 58 (62, 66, 70) sc.

Next row: Sc in each sc across.

Rep last row until piece measures 2½" from beg.

Dec: On next row, dec 1 st at each side as follows: Work 1 sc, sc2tog, sc to last 3 sts, sc2tog, 1 sc. Rep dec on every 4th row 2 more times = 52 (56, 60, 64) sc.

Work even until piece measures 6 (6¼, 7, 7¼)".

Inc: Inc 1 st at each side as follows: Work 1 sc, 2 sc in next st, sc to last 2 sts, 2 sc in next st, 1 sc. Rep dec on every 6th row 2 more times = 58 (62, 66, 70). Work even until piece measures 11½ (11¾, 13, 14)".

Armholes: Sl st across first 8 (10, 10, 11) sts, sc to last 8 (10, 10, 11) sts = 42 (42, 46, 48) sc. Turn and cont until piece measures 17 (17¾, 19, 21)".

Back straps: Work 1 sc in first 8 (8, 9, 9) sts, turn. Work in sc until strap measures ¾". Make another strap the same way on the opposite side.

Front

Work as for back until piece measures 15¾ (16½, 17¾, 19¾)".

Front straps: Work 1 sc in first 8 (8, 9, 9) sts. Turn and cont until piece measures 17¾ (18½, 19¾, 21¾)" from beg. Make another strap the same way on the opposite side.

Finishing

Sew shoulder and side seams. Work a rnd of sc around neck and armholes. Weave in ends.

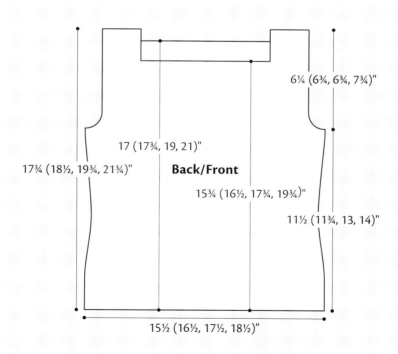

6¼ (6¾, 6¾, 7¾)"

17 (17¾, 19, 21)"

17¾ (18½, 19¾, 21¾)"

Back/Front

15¾ (16½, 17¾, 19¾)"

11½ (11¾, 13, 14)"

15½ (16½, 17½, 18½)"

V-NECK TOP

This top is simple and easy to make. You just make two pieces and then sew them together at the center front, center back, and sides.

Finished Measurements

Bust: 32 (37, 42)"

Length: 21½ (22, 22½)"

Materials

250 (300, 350) g; 680 (810, 956) yds of light worsted–weight merino wool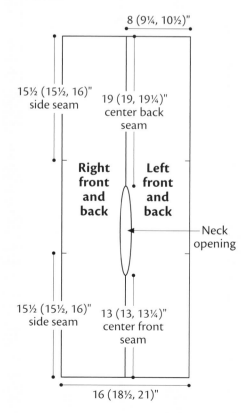

4 mm crochet hook

Gauge

13 sts and 9 rows = 4" in dc

Left Front and Back

At end of every row, turn and ch 3 (counts as 1 dc).

Ch 29 (33, 37). Dc in 4th ch from hook and in each dc across = 26 (30, 34) dc. Work in dc until piece measures 43 (44, 45)".

Right Front and Back

Work as for left back and front.

Finishing

Crochet the pieces tog with sl st seam (see page 93). For center-front seam, start at lower edge and sew seam for 13 (13, 13¼)". For center-back seam, start at lower edge and sew seam for 19 (19, 19¼)". Sew side seams for 15½ (15½, 16)" from lower edge to armhole.

Weave in ends.

8 (9¼, 10½)"

15½ (15½, 16)"
side seam

19 (19, 19¼)"
center back
seam

Right front and back

Left front and back

Neck opening

15½ (15½, 16)"
side seam

13 (13, 13¼)"
center front
seam

16 (18½, 21)"

A-LINE SKIRT

Pair the sleeveless top on page 36 with a cute skirt striped in the same color.

Finished Measurements

Waist: 29½ (32½, 39½)" (do not stretch when measuring)

Length: 17½ (18½, 19½)"

Circumference at hem: 61¼ (65½, 74)"

Materials

300 (400, 480) g; 820 (1,090; 1,312) yds of light worsted–weight merino wool in beige 3

50 (50, 60) g; 136 (136, 164) yds of light worsted–weight merino wool in natural white for stripe 3

4 mm crochet hook

4" long zipper (or longer zipper trimmed to fit; see page 93)

¾"-wide nonrolling elastic to fit waist

Removable stitch marker

Gauge

18 sts and 19 rows = 4" in sc (unstretched)

15 sts and 9 rows = 4" in dc

Waistband

Band is worked in a long strip of sc. For all 3 sizes, ch 21. Sc in 2nd ch from hook and in each sc across = 20 sc. Turn and ch 1 at end of every row. Cont rows in sc until you've worked a total of 140 (156, 188) rows or approx 29½ (32½, 39½)". Do not cut yarn, turn, ch 3, and beg skirt.

Skirt

At the end of every rnd, join with sl st in top of turning ch and ch 3 (counts as 1 dc).

Work 1 dc for every row along the long edge of the waistband = 140 (156, 188) sts. Join into rnd, ch 3. Pm to indicate center back and move marker up with each rnd. Work inc on every other rnd (beg at center back) as follows:

First inc rnd: Work 15 (17, 21) dc, 2 dc in next st, 19 (21, 25) dc, 2 dc in next st, 19 (21, 25) dc, 2 dc in next st, 28 (32, 40) dc, 2 dc in next st, 19 (21, 25) dc, 2 dc in next st, 19 (21, 25) dc, 2 dc in next st, 15 (17, 21) dc = 146 (162, 194) dc.

Second inc rnd: Work 15 (17, 21) dc, 2 dc in next st, 20 (22, 26) dc, 2 dc in next st, 20 (22, 26) dc, 2 dc in next st, 30 (34, 42) dc, 2 dc in next st, 20 (22, 26) dc, 2 dc in next st, 20 (22, 26) dc, 2 dc in next st, 15 (17, 21) dc = 152 (168, 200) dc.

Third inc rnd: Work 15 (17, 21) dc, 2 dc in next st, 21 (23, 27) dc, 2 dc in next st, 22 (24, 28) dc, 2 dc in next st, 30 (34, 42) dc, 2 dc in next st, 22 (24, 28) dc, 2 dc in next st, 21 (23, 27) dc, 2 dc in next st, 15 (17, 21) dc = 158 (174, 206) dc.

Fourth inc rnd: Work 15 (17, 21) dc, 2 dc in next st, 23 (25, 29) dc, 2 dc in next st, 23 (25, 29) dc, 2 dc in next st, 30 (34, 42) dc, 2 dc in next st, 23 (25, 29) dc, 2 dc in next st, 23 (25, 29) dc, 2 dc in next st, 15 (17, 21) dc = 164 (180, 212) dc.

Cont inc on every other rnd as established, working inc only at sides; center front and back remains straight from this point forward. AT THE SAME TIME, when skirt measures 11 (12, 13)" from waistband, work stripes: 1 rnd with natural white, 1 rnd beige, 1 rnd natural white, and 2 rnds beige.

Weave in ends.

Finishing

Sew zipper into waistband at center back. Sew elastic to WS of waistband. With yarn threaded on a tapestry needle and working on the inside of the waistband, create a pattern of Vs and upside down Vs as shown below. Insert elastic band into the framework you have just created, and sew the ends to secure.

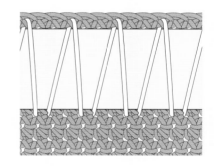

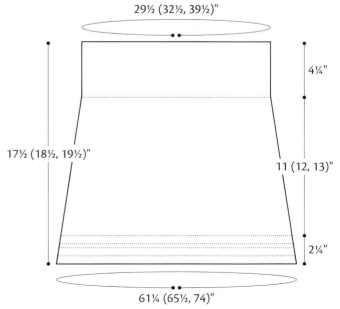

29½ (32½, 39½)"

4¼"

17½ (18½, 19½)"

11 (12, 13)"

2¼"

61¼ (65½, 74)"

KID MOHAIR VEST

This super easy and feminine vest looks sweet layered over a summer top or under a cardigan. The vest is held at the front with a pin or piece of jewelry.

Finished Measurements

Bust: 32 (33½, 38½)"
Length: 19½ (20, 20½)"

Materials

30 (40, 53) g; 290 (390, 514) yds of super fine–weight kid mohair 🧶1

6 mm crochet hook

Gauge

3 shells and 6 rows = 4"

Shell Pattern

Shell: Work (2 dc, ch 1, 2 dc) in ch-1 sp.

Row 1: Work shell in 4th st of previous row, *sk 4 sts, work shell in next st*; rep from * to * across. End with 1 dc in last st. Turn and ch 3.

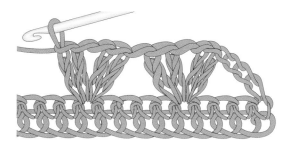

Row 2: Work shell in ch-1 sp of each shell on previous row. End with 1 dc in top of turning ch. Turn and ch 3.

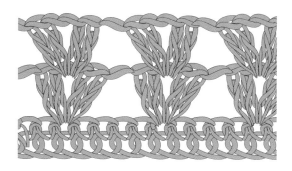

Rep row 2 for patt.

Back and Fronts

Vest is worked in shell pattern in one piece from the top down.

At end of every row, turn and ch 3 (counts as 1 dc).

Ch 92 (97, 107). Sc in 2nd ch from hook and in each ch across = 91 (96, 106) sc. Turn and ch 3.

Row 1: Work row 1 of shell patt = 18 (19, 21) shells.

Row 2 (inc row): Work 4 shells, (2 dc, ch 1, 2 dc, ch 1, 2 dc) in next ch-1 sp; cont in patt until 5 shells rem, work (2 dc, ch 1, 2 dc, ch 1, 2 dc) in next ch-1 sp, work 5 shells = 20 (21, 23) shells. End with 1 dc in turning ch.

Rows 3 and 5: (2 dc, ch 1, 2 dc) in each ch-1 sp across. End with 1 dc in turning ch.

Row 4 (inc row): Work 5 shells, (2 dc, ch 1, 2 dc) between next 2 shells; cont in patt until 5 shells rem, (2 dc, ch 1, 2 dc) between next 2 shells, work 5 shells = 22 (23, 25) shells. End with 1 dc in turning ch.

Row 6 (inc row): Work 5 shells, (2 dc, ch 1, 2 dc, ch 1, 2 dc) in next ch-1 sp; cont in patt until 6 shells rem, (2 dc, ch 1, 2 dc, ch 1, 2 dc) in next ch-1 sp, work 5 shells = 24 (25, 27) shells. End with 1 dc in turning ch.

Row 7: Rep row 3.

Shape armholes:

Row 1: Work 4 shells, ch 19 (24, 29), sk 4 shells, and cont in patt until 8 shells rem, ch 19 (24, 29), sk 4 shells, and cont in patt to end of row.

Row 2: Work 4 shells, *sk 4 ch, work (2 dc, ch 1, 2 dc) in next ch*; rep from * to * 2 (3, 4) more times. Cont in patt until reaching the 19 (24, 29) ch sts, sk 4 ch, **work (2 dc, ch 1, 2 dc) in next ch, sk 4 ch**. Work from ** to ** 2 (3, 4) more times and then cont in patt to end of row = 22 (25, 29) shells. End with 1 dc in turning ch.

Cont in patt without further shaping until piece measures 19½ (20, 20½)".

Weave in ends.

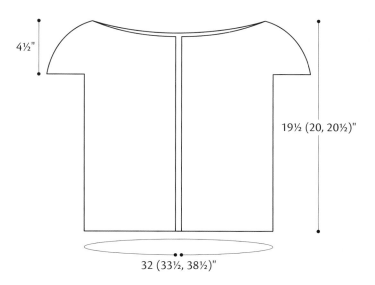

4½"

19½ (20, 20½)"

32 (33½, 38½)"

THREE-TIER SKIRT

This flirty, feminine skirt is easy to make and looks equally great at the beach or in town.

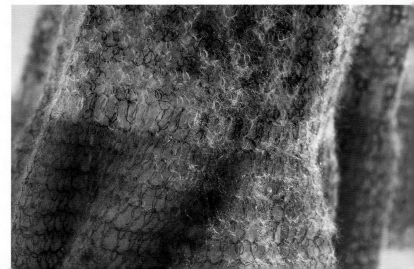

Finished Measurements

Waist: Gather waist to fit as desired by adjusting elastic length when finishing.

Hips: 31 (40, 45)"

Length: 21¾ (24½, 27½)"

Materials

Fine-weight mohair/polyester blend in the following amounts and colors: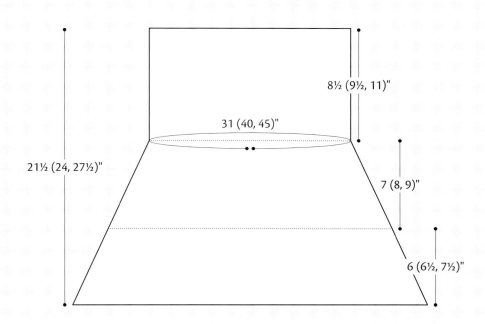

- **Top section:** 75 (75, 150) g; 820 (820, 1640) yds of medium blue
- **Middle section:** 50 (50, 100) g; 540 (540; 1,080) yds of multicolored blue
- **Bottom section:** 25 (50, 75) g; 270 (540, 820) yds of royal blue

3 mm, 6 mm, and 9 mm crochet hooks

½"-wide nonrolling elastic to fit waist

Gauge

18 sts and 23 rows = 4" in sc with smallest hook

Top Section

With 3 mm hook and medium blue, loosely ch 141 (180, 204). Join into a ring with sl st.

Work in sc around until piece measures 8½ (9½, 11)".

Ch 3 and work 1 rnd in dc.

Middle Section

Change to 6 mm hook and multicolored yarn.

Work (2 sc, 2 sc in next st) around = 188 (240, 272) sts.

Work even in sc for 7 (8, 9)".

Ch 3 and work 1 rnd in dc.

Bottom Section

Change to 9 mm hook and royal blue.

Small and Large: Work 2 sc, (2 sc, 2 sc in next st) around = 250 (362) sts.

Medium: Work (2 sc, 2 sc in next st) around = (320) sts.

Work even in sc for 6 (6½, 7½)".

Finishing

Fold ¾" to wrong side at waist and sew edge around, leaving a small opening. Insert elastic into waistband, secure ends of elastic, and close opening. Weave in ends.

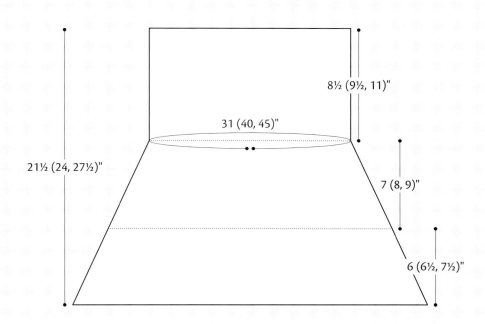

8½ (9½, 11)"

31 (40, 45)"

21½ (24, 27½)"

7 (8, 9)"

6 (6½, 7½)"

SUMMER TOP
WITH SHOULDER BANDS

*Keep cool in this summer top. It's so easy to make,
you'll want one in all your favorite colors.*

Finished Measurements

Bust: 32 (36, 40, 44)"

Length: 17½ (18½, 19½, 20)"

Materials

200 (250, 300, 330) g; 546 (656, 765, 875) yds of worsted-weight cotton (4)

4.5 mm crochet hook

Removable stitch marker

Gauge

14 sts and 16 rows = 4"

Pattern

Single crochet (sc) worked in back loop only, unless otherwise instructed.

Shoulder Bands

Top is worked in the round from the top down.

Ch 120 (134, 148, 162). Join into a ring with sl st and ch 1. Place removable marker in last st of rnd and move up with each rnd.

Work 1 rnd of sc in both loops.

Cont around in spiral, working sc into back loop only, for 2½ (2½, 2½, 3)".

Armholes

On next rnd, cont in patt, *sc 37 (43, 49, 55), ch 19 (20, 21, 22), sk 23 (24, 25, 29) sts, rep from * once = 112 (126, 140, 154) sts. Take all subsequent measurements from this point.

Back and Front

Cont in patt on 112 (126, 140, 154) sts until piece measures 2 (2, 2, 2½)". Pm at each side seam.

Dec: Cont in patt and AT THE SAME TIME dec 1 st on each side of marker at side seams on every 6th rnd 4 times (4-st dec each rnd) = 96 (110, 124, 138) sts.

Cont even in patt until piece measures 8½ (9½, 10, 10½)".

Inc: Cont in patt and AT THE SAME TIME inc 1 st on each side of marker at side seams on every 4th rnd 4 times (4-st inc each rnd) = 112 (126, 140, 154) sts.

Cont even in patt until piece measures 15 (16, 17, 17)".

Weave in ends.

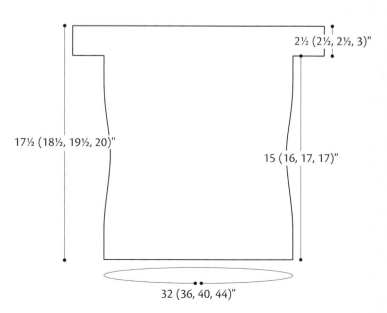

2½ (2½, 2½, 3)"

17½ (18½, 19½, 20)"

15 (16, 17, 17)"

32 (36, 40, 44)"

WRAPAROUND SKIRT

*A super simple cover-up
is perfect for the beach
or a pool party.*

Finished Measurements

Width at waist: 40 (48, 54)" (tie to fit waist)

Length: 14 (16, 17)"

Width at hem: 36 (43, 48½)"

Materials

Light worsted–weight cotton/rayon blend in
the following amounts and colors: (3)

Blue	100 (100, 133) g;	350 (350, 464) yds
Beige	100 (100, 110) g;	350 (350, 382) yds
Green	50 (100, 100) g;	175 (350, 350) yds
Yellow	50 (50, 50) g;	175 (175, 175) yds

4 mm crochet hook

Removable stitch markers

Gauge

20 sts and 16 rows = 4" in patt

Stitch Pattern

Row 1: Sc across, turn, and ch 2.

Row 2: Dc across, turn, and ch 1.

Rep rows 1 and 2 for patt.

1 row blue, 3 rows beige, 1 row yellow

2 rows green, 2 rows blue, 2 rows beige

2 rows blue, 2 rows green, 1 row yellow

1 row beige, 2 rows blue, 2 rows green

1 row yellow, 1 row beige, 2 rows green

1 row blue, 1 row yellow, 1 row beige

2 rows blue

Skirt

With green, ch 201 (241, 271). Sc in 2nd ch from hook and in each ch across = 200 (240, 270) sts.

Beg stripe sequence and work until piece measures 11 (12¾, 13)".

Place markers on next row at 10¾ (12¾, 13)", 14½ (16½, 17)", 24¾ (30¾, 37)", and 28¾ (34¾, 41)".

Beg dec: Dec 1 st at each marker on all sc rows (4-st dec) until piece measures 14 (16, 17)".

Work 1 row of sc with blue along 2 short sides.

Cord: Holding 1 strand of each color tog, make 2 crochet chains, one about 25½" and the other 45¼" long. Sew a cord to each side of skirt at top.

Cord loops: Make loops over the 2 center dec lines as follows: attach yarn at edge and work 1 sc, ch for ¾", and attach ch about ¾" below edge.

Finishing

Weave in ends. Thread the cords through the loops and tie at front.

Stripe Sequence

2 rows blue, 2 rows beige, 1 row yellow

3 rows blue, 2 rows green, 3 rows beige

1 row yellow, 2 rows blue, 2 rows green

2 rows beige, 2 rows blue, 2 rows yellow

2 rows beige, 2 rows green, 4 rows blue

2 rows beige, 2 rows green, 1 row yellow

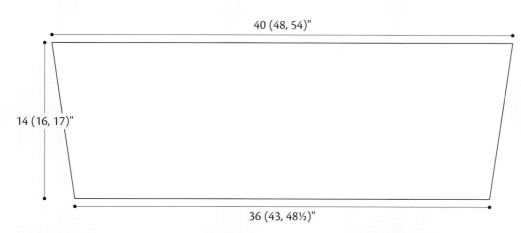

HALTER TOP

Paired with jeans or a skirt, this halter looks great and keeps you cool.

Finished Measurements

Bust: Approx 27½ (31½, 35½)"

Length at side seam: 11½ (12, 12½)"

Materials

150 (150, 200) g; 262 (262, 350) yds of worsted-weight cotton (4)

4.5 mm crochet hook

Elastic cord, 27½ (31½, 35½)" long, in color to match yarn

Removable stitch markers

Gauge

12 sts and 7 rows = 4" in dc

Body

Ch 80 (92, 104). Join into a ring with sl st and ch 2. Place removable marker in last st of rnd and move up with each rnd. Marker at beg of rnd indicates side seam.

Join every rnd with sl st and ch 2.

Dc in each ch around.

Working in back loops only, dc around until piece measures 11½ (12, 12½)"; cut yarn.

V-Neck Top

Work rows of sc in both loops.

At end of every row, turn and ch 1.

Row 1: Attach yarn in 9th (11th, 13th) st before marker. Work in sc on next 58 (68, 78) sts, turn, and ch 1.

Row 2 (inc): Work 19 (22, 26) sc, 2 sc in each of next 2 sts (2-st inc), 16 (20, 22) sc, 2 sc in each of next 2 sts (2-st inc), 19 (22, 26) sc = 62 (72, 82) sts. Pm between 2 inc sts to indicate bust dart.

Row 3 (dec): Dec 1 st at each side and inc at bust darts as follows: work 1 sc, sc2tog, sc to 1 st before marked dart, 2 sc in each of next 2 sts, sc to 1 st before next marker for dart, 2 sc in each of next 2 sts, sc to last 3 sts, sc2tog, 1 sc = 64 (74, 84) sts.

Rep row 3 another 4 (5, 6) times = 72 (84, 96) sts after last row.

Rows 8 (9, 10): Discontinue inc, but cont 1 dec at each side as established = 70 (82, 94) sts.

Rep last row 1 (2, 3) more times = 68 (78, 88) sts.

Pm to indicate center-front, 34 (39, 44) sts on each side. Work each side separately.

Next row: *Work 1 sc, sc2tog, sc to 3 sts before marker, sc2tog, 1 sc, turn, and ch 1 = 32 (37, 42) sts.

Rep last row until 4 (5, 6) sts rem. Do not cut yarn.

Work even until strap measures approx 9" to 9¾".* Do not cut yarn until second strap is completed and you've tried top on.

With second ball of yarn, attach yarn at center front and work from * to * for other side.

Try top on to make sure straps fit comfortably, and adjust as needed. Join ends of strap tog at center back.

Finishing

Sew elastic cord on row between dc and sc sections and along back. Weave in ends.

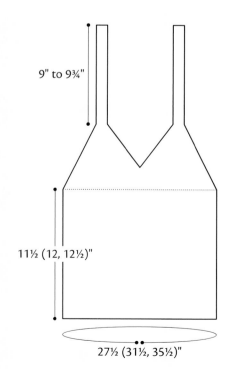

9" to 9¾"

11½ (12, 12½)"

27½ (31½, 35½)"

FISHNET STOCKINGS

Your crocheted silk stockings will become legendary.
Wear them for everyday with boots or to parties
with fancy high heels. The stockings can be held up by
garters or with thin elastic attached to the upper edge.

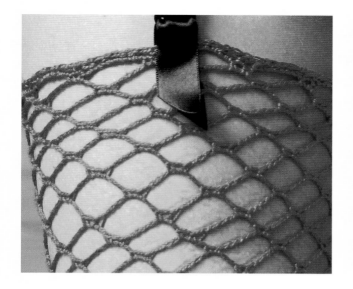

Finished Measurements (see note below)

Foot circumference: 7"

Leg length: 33½"

Materials

100 g; 656 yds of super fine–weight silk

2.5 mm crochet hook

Stitch marker

Gauge

8 loops wide and 14 loops long = 4"

NOTE: It will be difficult to measure the gauge accurately, so try the stockings on periodically as you work. You can make a larger size by working one more chain stitch in each loop.

Toe

Ch 6 and join into a ring with 1 sl st, ch 2.

Rnd 1: Work 15 dc in ring. Join with sl st, ch 2.

Rnd 2: Work 2 dc in each st = 30 sts. Join with sl st, ch 2.

Rnd 3: Work 2 dc in each st = 60 sts. Join with sl st.

Net Patt

Rnd 1: *Ch 5, sk 3 sts, work 1 sc*; rep from * to * around = 15 loops.

Mark beg of rnd and cont to work around in a spiral: *ch 5, 2 sc in loop*; rep from * to * until there are 90 loops in length.

Work 12 rnds with (ch 6, 2 sc) in each loop.

Work 12 rnds with (ch 7, 2 sc) in each loop = 114 loops total in length.

Edging

Work *7 sc in ch loop, sk 1 st, 1 sc*; rep from * to * around, join with sl st. Ch 1 and work 1 sc in each st around.

Make other stocking the same way. Weave in ends.

SLEEVELESS TOP

This long top has a dense lower edge. For a comfortably chic look, pair it with jeans.

Finished Measurements

Bust: 32 (36, 41)"

Length: 33½ (33½, 34½)"

Circumference at hem: 27 (31, 34)"

Materials

400 (500, 600) g; 918 (1,148; 1, 370) yds of worsted-weight acrylic/polyester blend (4)

6 mm and 8 mm crochet hooks

Gauge

13 sts and 18 rows = 4" in sc with smaller hook

11 sts and 5 rows = 4" in dc with larger hook

Back

At end of every sc row, turn and ch 1.

At end of every dc row, turn and ch 3 (counts as 1 dc).

Ch 45 (51, 57) with smaller hook; turn and ch 1. Sc in 2nd ch from hook and in each ch across = 44 (50, 56) sts.

Work in rows of sc until piece measures 9½ (9½, 10)". At end of last row, turn and ch 3.

Dc in next st and in each sc across = 44 (50, 56) dc.

Change to larger hook, cont in rows of dc until piece measures 33½ (33½, 34½)".

Front

Work as for back.

Finishing

For each shoulder, join 1¼ (1¼, 1½)" along top edge. For each armhole, sew 25½" side seams. Weave in ends.

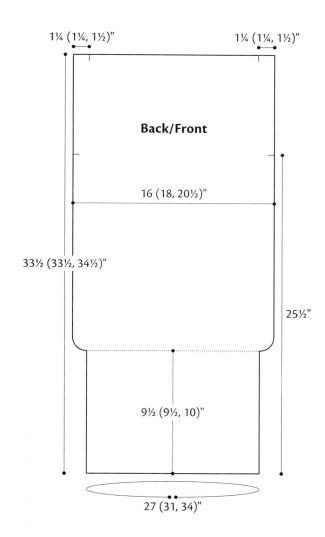

1¼ (1¼, 1½)" 1¼ (1¼, 1½)"

Back/Front

16 (18, 20½)"

33½ (33½, 34½)"

25½"

9½ (9½, 10)"

27 (31, 34)"

MOHAIR TOP,
WITH OR WITHOUT SLEEVES

*Customize this open and airy design by
making the topper's sleeves long or short,
or omit the sleeves altogether for a vest.*

Finished Measurements

Bust: 32 (34, 36, 40)"

Length to neck: 22 (23, 23½, 24½)"

Materials

Top: 50 (75, 75, 100) g; 546 (820, 820; 1,100) yds of fine-weight kid mohair (**2**)

Vest: 50 (50, 50, 75) g; 546 (546, 546, 820) yds of fine-weight kid mohair (**2**)

8 mm crochet hook

Removable stitch markers

Gauge

8 sts and 6 rows = 4" in dc

Back

At end of every row, turn and ch 2 (counts as 1 st).

With 2 strands of yarn held tog, ch 34 (36, 38, 42). Drop 1 strand. Dc in 3rd ch from hook and in each ch across = 32 (34, 36, 40) dc.

Work in dc with 1 strand of yarn until piece measures 15 (15½, 15½, 16)".

Armholes: Sl 2 sts, work to last 2 sts, turn and ch 2 = 28 (30, 32, 36) sts. Work even until piece measures 7 (7½, 8, 8½)" from beg of armhole. Place a marker at each side to indicate beg of collar.

Rolled collar: Work even until collar measures 12", or until entire piece measures 34 (35, 35½, 36½)".

Front

Work as for back.

Sleeves

Omit sleeves for vest.

At end of every row, turn and ch 2 (counts as 1 st).

With 2 strands of yarn held tog, ch 23 (23, 25, 25). Drop 1 strand. Dc in 3rd ch from hook and in each ch across = 21 (21, 23, 23) dc.

Work in dc with 1 strand of yarn, inc 1 st at each side on every 5th row, until there are a total of 27 (29, 31, 33) sts.

Work even until sleeve measures 19½".

Finishing

Sew side seams up to underarm. Seam collar tog, beg at marker. For top with sleeves: sew sleeve seams except for the top 1". Sew sleeves into armhole. Sew remainder of sleeve seams to slipped sts at underarm. Weave in ends.

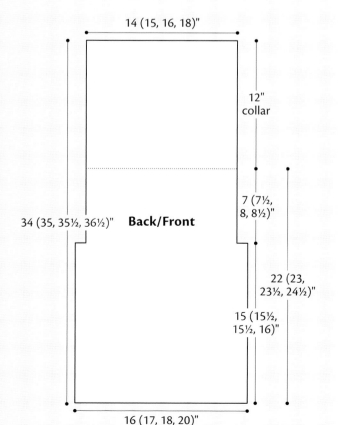

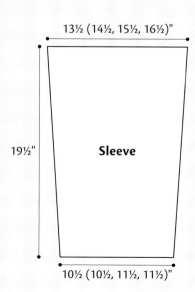

WIDE-NECK TOP

This simple top features raglan sleeves and a lovely neckline that can be pulled down over one shoulder.

Finished Measurements

Bust: 34 (38, 42)"

Length: 19½ (20, 22)"

Materials

250 (300, 350) g; 1,367 (1,650, 1,900) yds of super fine–weight baby alpaca (**1**)

4 mm crochet hook

Gauge

18 sts and 14 rows = 4" in st patt

Stitch Pattern

Row 1: Work 1 sc in each st (work somewhat tightly); turn with ch 2.

Row 2: *Work 1 dc in second st of previous row, 1 dc in first st of previous row*; rep from * to * across (work this row loosely). End with 1 dc in turning ch; turn with ch 1.

Rep rows 1 and 2. The crossed dc should be stacked one above the other.

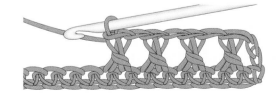

Back

With 2 strands of yarn held tog, ch 78 (88, 96) loosely. Drop 1 strand of yarn and beg st patt, starting row 1 with sc in 2nd ch from hook = 77 (87, 95) sts. Cont in patt until piece measures 4". End with completed row 2.

Dec: On next sc row, dec as follows: work 1 sc, sc2tog twice, sc to last 5 sts, sc2tog twice, 1 sc. Rep dec row on sc rows a total of 4 times = 61 (71, 79) sc.

Cont in st patt without further shaping until piece measures 9 (9, 9½)". End with completed row 2.

Inc: On next sc row, inc as follows: work 1 sc, (2 sc in next st) twice, sc to last 3 sts, (2 sc in next st) twice, 1 sc. Rep inc row on every other sc row a total of 4 times = 77 (87, 95) sc.

Cont in st patt without further shaping until piece measures 15 (15, 17)". End with completed row 2.

Armholes: Sl st across first 6 (6, 8) sts, sc across until 6 (6, 8) sts rem; turn = 65 (75, 79) sts.

Raglan shaping: Dec 2 sts at each side on sc rows as above 7 (8, 8) times = 37 (43, 47) sts.

Front

Work as for back.

Sleeves

Ch 52. Beg st patt, starting row 1 of patt with sc in 2nd ch from hook, and work in patt for 4 (4, 4)" = 51 sts. End with completed row 2.

On next sc row, inc 2 sts at each side as for back, and rep inc on every 8th row until there are 63 (67, 71) sts.

Cont in st patt without further shaping until sleeve measures 19½ (19½, 20)". End with completed row 2.

Armholes: Sl st across first 6 (6, 8) sts, sc across until 6 (6, 8) sts rem; turn = 51 (55, 55).

Raglan shaping: Dec 2 sts at each side on sc rows as for back 7 (8, 8) times = 23 sts.

Finishing

Join raglan seams and sew side seams. Work 1 rnd of sc around neck. Weave in ends.

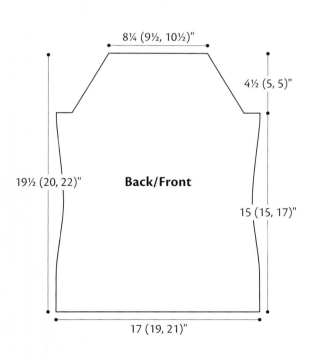

8¼ (9½, 10½)"

4½ (5, 5)"

19½ (20, 22)"

Back/Front

15 (15, 17)"

17 (19, 21)"

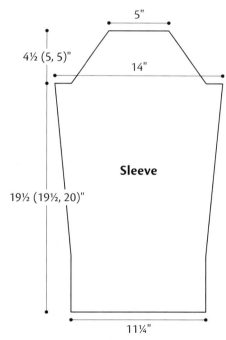

5"

4½ (5, 5)"

14"

Sleeve

19½ (19½, 20)"

11¼"

TWO-COLOR
MOHAIR SWEATER

This pink-and-orange sweater is as pretty as a sunset. Extralong sleeves and a rolled collar that stands up are special features.

Finished Measurements

Bust: 37 (41, 43)"

Length to beg of collar: 22½ (23½, 24½)"

Materials

200 (250, 300) g; 634 (792, 984) yds of light worsted–weight mohair in pink [3]

100 (100, 120) g; 317 (317, 382) yds of light worsted–weight mohair in orange [3]

8 mm crochet hook

Gauge

9 sts and 13 rows = 4" in sc

Back

At end of every row, turn and ch 1.

With orange, ch 43 (47, 50). Work 1 row in sc, beg in 2nd ch from hook = 42 (46, 49) sc.

Work in sc until piece measures 4 (4¼, 5)".

Dec: On next row, dec 1 st at each side as follows: work 1 sc, sc2tog, sc to last 3 sts, sc2tog, 1 sc. Rep dec on every 4th row a total of 3 times = 36 (40, 43) sts.

Work even until piece measures 8 (8¼, 9½)".

Change to pink and work 2 rows in sc.

Inc: On next row, inc 1 st at each side as follows: work 1 sc, 2 sc in next st, sc to last 2 sts, 2 sc in next st, 1 sc. Rep inc every 6 (6, 5) rows a total of 3 (3, 3) times = 42 (46, 49) sts.

Work even until piece measures 14½ (15, 15½)".

Armholes: Sl st across first 3 sts, sc to last 3 sts, turn, and ch 1 = 36 (40, 43) sts. Work 1 row even.

Raglan shaping: Dec 1 st at each side as above on every other row 8 (9, 10) times. Then dec 1 st at each side every 4 rows 2 times = 16 (18, 19) sts. For Large only, work 1 row even.

Front

Work as for back.

Sleeves

With pink, ch 21 (23, 25). Work sc in 2nd ch from hook and in each ch across = 20 (22, 24) sc.

Work in sc until sleeve measures 6".

Inc: On next row, inc 1 st at each side as for back, and rep inc every 6 (6, 8) rows a total of 6 times = 32 (34, 40) sts.

Work even until sleeve measures 21½".

Armholes: Sl st across first 3 sts, sc to last 3 sts, turn, and ch 1 = 26 (28, 34) sts. Work 1 row even.

Raglan shaping: Dec 1 st at each side as for back raglan on every other row 8 (9, 10) times. Then dec 1 st at each side every 4 rows 2 times = 6 (6, 10) sts.

Finishing

Sew raglan seams tog and then sew sleeve and side seams.

Collar: Join pink at center-back neck and sc 44 (48, 50) sts evenly around neck. End each rnd with a sl st in first st on previous rnd and ch 1. Work even until collar measures about 11¾".

Weave in ends.

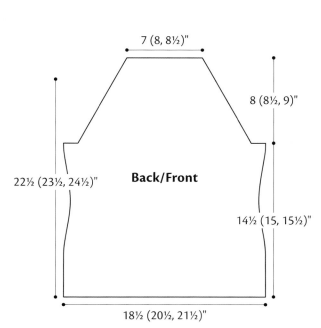

7 (8, 8½)"

8 (8½, 9)"

22½ (23½, 24½)"

Back/Front

14½ (15, 15½)"

18½ (20½, 21½)"

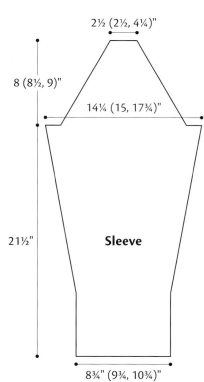

2½ (2½, 4¼)"

8 (8½, 9)"

14¼ (15, 17¾)"

21½"

Sleeve

8¾ (9¾, 10¾)"

V-NECK SWEATER

This easy sweater is done in single crochet.

Finished Measurements

Bust: 32 (34, 38, 40)"
Length: 23 (23½, 24, 24½)"

Materials

350 (400, 450, 500) g; 612 (700, 786, 875) yds of bulky-weight cotton (5)
6 mm crochet hook
Removable stitch marker (size Medium only)

Gauge

14 sts and 12 rows = 4"

Back

At end of every row, turn and ch 1.

Ch 57 (61, 67, 71). Sc in 2nd ch from hook and in each sc across = 56 (60, 66, 70) sc.

Work in sc until piece measures 4".

Dec: Dec 1 st at each side as follows: work 1 sc, sc2tog, sc to last 3 sts, sc2tog, 1 sc. Rep dec every other row a total of 4 times = 48 (52, 58, 62) sc.

Work even until piece measures 13".

Inc: Inc 1 st at each side as follows: work 1 sc, 2 sc in next st, sc to last 2 sts, 2 sc in next st, 1 sc. Rep inc every other row a total of 4 times = 56 (60, 66, 70) sc.

Work even until piece measures 15½ (15½, 16, 16)".

Armholes: Dec 1 st at each side as above every other row 8 (9, 10, 10) times = 40 (42, 46, 50) sc.

Work even until piece measures 23 (23½, 24, 24½)".

Front

Work as for back until front measures 15¾", ending with WS row. On last row, place removable marker between sts 28 and 29 (30 and 31, 33 and 32, 35 and 36). Work front for V-neck shaping as follows and AT THE SAME TIME shape armholes as for back:

First side of V-neck: Dec 1 st at neck edge as follows: sc to last 3 sts before marker, sc2tog, sc 1. Turn, ch 1, and sc across. Rep dec on every other row a total of 11 (12, 12, 10) times. Work armhole dec as for back = 9 (9, 11, 15) sts rem after all dec. Work even until piece measures 23 (23½, 24, 24½)".

Second side of V-neck: Attach yarn at center and work neck dec as follows: 1 sc, sc2tog, sc across row. Rep dec on every other row a total of 11 (12, 12, 10) times. Work armhole dec as for back = 9 (9, 11, 15) sts rem after all dec.

Work even until piece measures 23 (23½, 24, 24½)".

Sleeves

Ch 31 (33, 35, 35). Sc in 2nd ch from hook and in each sc across = 30 (32, 34, 34) sc.

Work in sc until sleeve measures 4".

Inc row: Work inc as for back and rep inc on every 8th row until there are 38 (42, 46, 48) sts.

Work even until sleeve measures 19½ (19½, 19½, 21)".

Sleeve cap: Dec 2 sts at each side on every other row 4 (5, 6, 7) times, and 1 st at each side every other row 4 (3, 2, 0) times = 14 (16, 18, 20) sts.

Finishing

Join shoulder seams. Attach sleeves. Sew sleeve and side seams. Weave in ends.

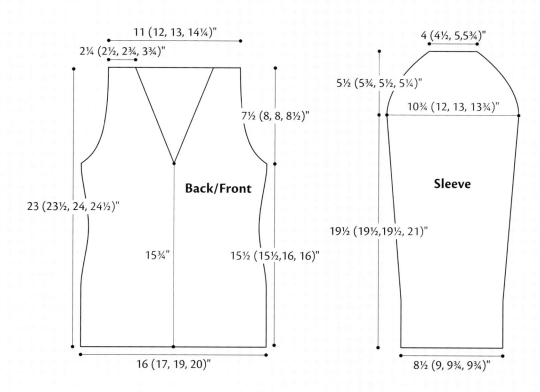

BUTTON-COLLAR SWEATER

Three buttons at the collar add flair to this comfortable sweater. Worked in single crochet, it's easy to make and the right weight for wearing year-round.

Finished Measurements

Bust: 32 (35, 38, 41½)"

Length: 20 (21, 22, 23)"

Materials

450 (500, 550, 600) g; 1,378 (1,530; 1,684; 1,860) yds of worsted-weight linen/polyester blend (**4**)

4 mm crochet hook

3 horn-shaped buttons, 1" long

Gauge

15 sts and 19 rows = 4"

Back

At end of every row, turn and ch 1.

Ch 61 (67, 73, 79). Sc in 2nd ch from hook and in each ch across = 60 (66, 72, 78) sc.

Work in sc until piece measures 4 (4¼, 4¾, 5¼)".

Dec: On next row, dec 1 st at each side as follows: work 1 sc, sc2tog, sc to last 3 sts, sc2tog, 1 sc. Rep dec every 4th row 2 more times = 54 (60, 66, 72) sts.

Work even until piece measures 8 (8¼, 8¾, 9)".

Inc: On next row, inc 1 st at each side as follows: work 1 sc, 2 sc in next st, sc to last 2 sts, 2 sc in next st, 1 sc. Rep inc on every 6th row 2 more times = 60 (66, 72, 78) sts.

Work even until piece measures 12½ (13, 13½, 14)".

Armholes: Dec for armholes as follows: sl 1 st, work to last st, leave rem st unworked, turn. Rep dec on every other row 4 more times = 50 (56, 62, 68) sts.

Work even until armhole measures 6½ (7, 7½, 8)".

Neck: Work 20 (22, 24, 26) sc, turn, sl 4 sts, and sc to end of row. Turn, work 16 (18, 20, 22) sc, turn, sl 4, and sc to end of row. Turn, work 12 (14, 16, 18) sc, and cut yarn. Armhole should measure 7½ (8, 8½, 9)". Sk 10 (12, 14, 16) sts for back neck, attach yarn in next st, and work 20 (22, 24, 26) sc. Turn, work 16 (18, 20, 22) sc, leaving 4 sts unworked; turn and sc to end of row. Turn, work 12 (14, 16, 18) sc, leaving 4 sts unworked; turn and sc to end of row.

Front

Work as for back until piece measures 12¾ (13, 13½, 14)".

Armholes: BO for armholes as follows: sl st in next 3 sts, sc to last 3 sts, leave rem sts unworked. (Sl st in first st, sc to last st, leave rem st unworked) on every other row twice = 50 (56, 62, 68) sts. Work even until piece measures 13¾ (14½, 15½, 15¾)".

Left side placket: Sc 27 (30, 33, 36) sts, turn. Work even for 1¼".

Buttonhole: Work until 4 sts rem at neck edge, ch 2, sk 2 sts, work 2 sc. On next row, work 2 sc in ch-2 sp. Work even until placket measures a total of 2½".

Left neck: Dec at neck on every other row as follows: Work to last 4 (5, 6, 7) sts, turn, work back. (Work to last 3 sts, turn, work back) twice. (Work to last 2 sts, turn, work back) twice. Work to last st, turn, work back = 12 (14, 16, 18) sts. Work until front is same length as back.

Right side placket: With new ball of yarn, ch 10 sts for facing at neck, sc across 23 (26, 29, 32) sts on right side of front = 33 (36, 39, 42) sts. Work for 2½" from neck edge to armhole.

Right neck: Sl sts at neck edge on every other row as follows: 10 (11, 12, 13) sts once, 3 sts twice, 2 sts twice, 1 st once = 12 (14, 16, 18) sts. Work until same length as back.

Left Sleeve

Ch 33 (35, 35, 37). Sc in 2nd ch from hook and in each ch across = 32 (34, 34, 36) sts.

Work in sc until sleeve measures 4".

Inc: On next row, inc 1 st at each side as follows: work 1 sc, 2 sc in next st, sc to last 2 sts, 2 sc in next st, 1 sc. Rep inc every 6 (6, 6, 5) rows until there are a total of 54 (56, 58, 60) sts.

Work even until sleeve is 19½ (19½, 19½, 18)" long.

Sleeve cap: Dec at both sides at the same time on every other row as follows: at beg of row (right side), sl required number of sts; at end of row (left side), work to required number of sts, turn. **For Extra Small, Small, and Medium,** at right side, dec 1 st 4 (5, 6) times, 2 sts twice, 3 sts 3 times. At left side, dec 5 (6, 7, 7) sts once, 3 sts twice, 1 st 4 times, 2 sts 4 times = 14 sts rem. **For Large,** at right side, dec 1 st 11 times, 2 sts 3 times. At left side, dec 7 sts once, 3 sts once, 1 st 8 times, 2 sts 4 times = 17 sts rem. For all sizes, work until sleeve cap measures 6 (6¼, 6¾, 7)".

Right Sleeve

Work as for left sleeve, reversing shaping.

Finishing

Sew all seams. Attach sleeves, joining the 5 (6, 7, 7) bound-off sts to front.

Collar: Pick up approx 76 (80, 84, 88) sts around neck. Work for 3¼", making 2 buttonholes as before, with approx 1½" between each buttonhole. Place the facing with the cast-on sts underneath and sew at base of placket. Sew on buttons.

Weave in ends.

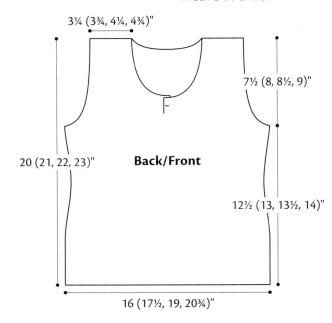

3¼ (3¾, 4¼, 4¾)"

7½ (8, 8½, 9)"

20 (21, 22, 23)"   **Back/Front**

12½ (13, 13½, 14)"

16 (17½, 19, 20¾)"

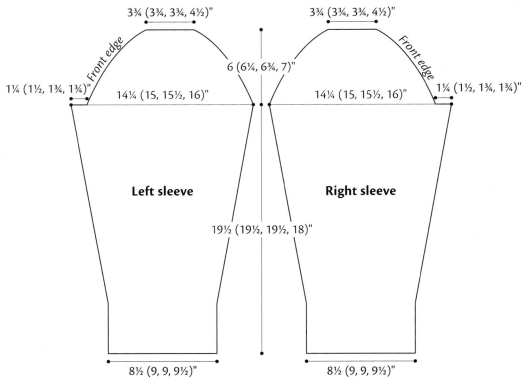

3¾ (3¾, 3¾, 4½)"   3¾ (3¾, 3¾, 4½)"

Front edge   *Front edge*

6 (6¼, 6¾, 7)"

1¼ (1½, 1¾, 1¾)"   14¼ (15, 15½, 16)"   14¼ (15, 15½, 16)"   1¼ (1½, 1¾, 1¾)"

Left sleeve   **Right sleeve**

19½ (19½, 19½, 18)"

8½ (9, 9, 9½)"   8½ (9, 9, 9½)"

DEEP V-NECK SWEATER WITH COLLAR

A plunging V-neck creates drama in this gorgeous sweater. Single crochet means it's easy to make and a mohair-wool blend makes it warm to wear.

Finished Measurements

Bust: 35½ (38, 42)"
Length: 23 (23½, 24)"

Materials

250 (300, 320) g; 792 (950; 1,010) yds of light worsted–weight kid mohair/wool blend **3**

8 mm crochet hook

Gauge

9 sts and 14 rows = 4"

Back

At end of every row, turn and ch 1.

Ch 41 (44, 48). Sc in 2nd ch from hook and in each ch across = 40 (43, 47) sc.

Work in sc until piece measures 4¾".

Dec: On next row, dec 1 st at each side as follows: work 1 sc, sc2tog, sc to last 3 sts, sc2tog, 1 sc. Rep dec every 4 rows 2 more times = 34 (37, 41) sts.

Work even until piece is 9½" long.

Inc: On next row, inc 1 st at each side as follows: work 1 sc, 2 sc in next st, sc to last 2 sts, 2 sc in next st, 1 sc. Rep inc every 6 rows 2 more times = 40 (43, 47) sts.

Work even until piece measures 15 (15½, 15½)".

Armholes: On next row, dec 1 st at each side as follows: work 1 sc, sc2tog, sc to last 3 sts, sc2tog, 1 sc. Rep dec on every other row 3 more times = 32 (35, 39) sts. Work even until armhole measures 7½ (7½, 8)".

Shoulders: Work 8 (8, 10) sts from side edge; turn and ch 1. Work 2 sl sts and 6 (6, 8) sc. Fasten off. Work other side to match, reversing shaping.

Front

Work as for back until piece measures 5½".

Left side: Work to center 4 (5, 5) sts; leave these sts unworked; turn and cont shaping at side and armhole as for back and AT THE SAME TIME dec 1 st (by working 1 sc, sc2tog at neck edge) every 6 rows at center-front edge until 6 (6, 8) sts rem. Work even until armhole is same length as for back.

Right side: Work as for left front, reversing shaping.

Sleeves

Ch 19 (21, 23). Sc in 2nd ch from hook and in each sc across = 18 (20, 22) sc.

Work in sc until sleeve measures 4".

Inc: On next row, inc 1 st at each side as follows: work 1 sc, 2 sc in next st, sc to last 2 sts, 2 sc in next st, 1 sc. Rep inc every 6 rows until there are 30 (34, 36) sts.

Work even until sleeve measures 19½ (19½, 19)".

Sleeve cap: On next row, dec 1 st at each side as follows: work 1 sc, sc2tog, sc to last 3 sts, sc2tog, 1 sc. Rep dec on every other row until 18 (20, 20) sts rem.

Finishing

Join shoulders. Attach sleeves and sew sleeve and side seams.

Collar: The collar is worked back and forth, beg at right shoulder seam. Work over back neck sts as follows: work 1 sc, 18 (21, 37) dc, 1 sc. *Turn, ch 1, work 1 sc in first st, dc to last st, work 1 sc in same loop as first sc of previous row. Cont with 1 dc in the same loop at the curve in the sweater neck (to avoid holes), work another 8 dc and 1 sc*.

Small and Medium only: Rep from * to * 7 times on each side. The last st is a dc.

Large only: Rep from * to * until sts are worked along entire right- and left-front edges. Note that you may not need as many inc sts in last 2 rows worked.

All sizes: There should now be 134 (147, 167) total sts and about 14 rows at the widest point. Turn, ch 2, and work in dc for 2". Overlap ends and join short ends of collar to 4 (5, 5) sts that were left unworked when you divided the front.

Weave in ends.

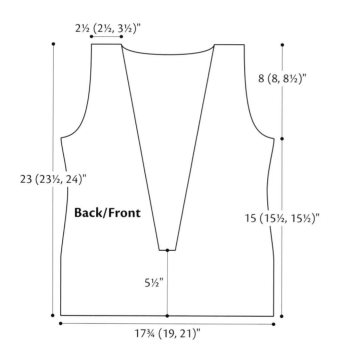

2½ (2½, 3½)"

8 (8, 8½)"

23 (23½, 24)"

Back/Front

15 (15½, 15½)"

5½"

17¾ (19, 21)"

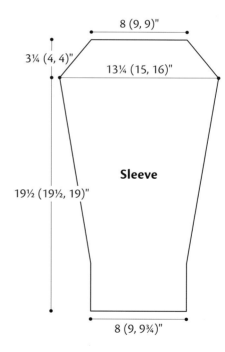

8 (9, 9)"

3¼ (4, 4)"

13¼ (15, 16)"

Sleeve

19½ (19½, 19)"

8 (9, 9¾)"

Wrap yourself in the ultimate luxury of kid mohair. This easy-to-crochet sweater is worked entirely in single crochet.

Finished Measurements

Bust: 32 (35, 38½, 42)"

Length: 20½ (21, 21½, 22)"

Materials

125 (150, 175, 200) g; 1,367 (1,640; 1,914; 2,180) yds of fine-weight kid mohair (⬤2)

5 mm crochet hook

Gauge

15 sts and 20 rows = 4"

Back

At end of every row, turn and ch 1.

Ch 61 (67, 73, 79). Sc in 2nd ch from hook and in each ch across = 60 (66, 72, 78).

Work in sc until piece measures 20½ (21, 21½, 22)".

Left Front and Tie

Ch 181 (191, 201, 221); turn and ch 1. Sc in 2nd ch from hook and in each ch across = 180 (190, 200, 220) sc.

Work in sc for 1¼".

BO for tie on left side: On every other row, sl 20 sts 4 (4, 5, 5) times, sl 10 sts 3 (3, 5, 5) times, sl 8 sts 3 (4, 0, 2) times = 46 (48, 50, 54) sts.

Shape V-neck: BO on same side as tie by dec 1 st on every 3rd row until 20 (24, 26, 29) sts rem; (work dec as follows: sl 1 st at neck edge, or work to neck edge until 1 st remains and turn). Work even until piece measures 20½ (21, 21½, 22)" at side seam.

Right Front and Tie

Work as for left front, but reverse shaping.

Sleeves

Ch 33 (35, 37, 37); turn and ch 1. Sc in 2nd ch from hook and in each ch across = 32 (34, 36, 36) sc.

Work in sc until sleeve measures 2".

Inc: On next row, inc 1 st at each side as follows: work 1 sc, 2 sc in next st, sc to last 2 sts, 2 sc in next st, 1 sc. Rep inc on every 8th row until there are 52 (56, 60, 64) sts.

Work even until sleeve measures 20½ (21, 21½, 21½)".

Finishing

Join shoulders. Attach sleeves and sew sleeve seams. Sew side seams, leaving a 1¼"-long opening for the tie on one side, approx 2¾" to 3¼" from the lower edge.

Weave in ends.

Edging: Work 1 row of sc around V-neck and along front edge of ties.

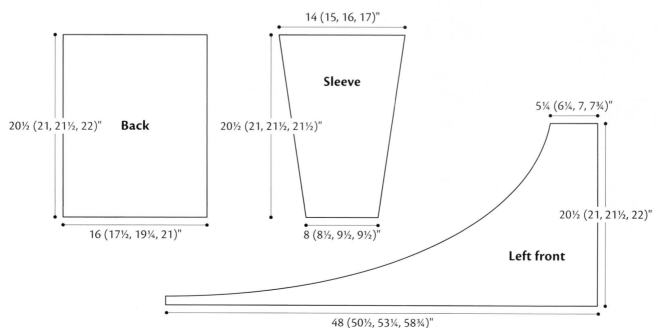

14 (15, 16, 17)"

Sleeve

20½ (21, 21½, 22)" **Back**

20½ (21, 21½, 21½)"

16 (17½, 19¼, 21)"

8 (8½, 9½, 9½)"

5¼ (6¼, 7, 7¾)"

20½ (21, 21½, 22)"

Left front

48 (50½, 53¼, 58¾)"

SWEATER
WITH WIDE COLLAR

The front, back, and sleeves of this sweater are made separately and then joined to create the yoke and wide collar.

Finished Measurements

Bust: 35½ (40½, 45½)"

Length to half of collar depth: 23½ (24½, 26½)"

Materials

A   125 (125 (150) g; 1,367 (1,367; 1,640) yds of fine-weight kid mohair **2**

B   200 (250, 300) g; 1,094 (1,367; 1,640) yds of fine-weight baby alpaca **2**

5 mm, 6 mm, and 7 mm crochet hooks

Removable stitch markers

Gauge

13 sts and 19 rows = 4" with 1 strand each of A and B held tog on 5 mm hook

Back

The sweater is worked with 1 strand each of A and B held tog throughout.

At end of every row, turn and ch 1.

With 5 mm hook, ch 59 (67, 75). Sc in 2nd ch from hook and in each ch across = 58 (66, 74) sc.

Work in sc until piece measures 4".

Dec: On next row, dec 1 st at each side as follows: work 1 sc, sc2tog, sc to last 3 sts, sc2tog, 1 sc. Rep dec every 4 (4, 5) rows 3 more times = 50 (58, 66) sts rem.

Work even until piece measures 9½".

Inc: On next row, inc 1 st at each side as follows: work 1 sc, 2 sc in next st, sc to last 2 sts, 2 sc in next st, 1 sc. Rep inc on every 6th row 3 more times = 58 (66, 74) sts.

Work even until piece measures 16 (16, 17)".

Front

Work as for back.

Sleeves

With 5 mm hook, ch 29 (31, 35). Sc in 2nd ch from hook and in each ch across = 28 (30, 34) sc.

Work in sc until sleeve measures 3¼".

Inc: On next row, inc 1 st at each side as follows: work 1 sc, 2 sc in next st, sc to last 2 sts, 2 sc in next st, 1 sc. Rep inc every 8 (6, 6) rows until there are a total of 46 (50, 54) sts.

Work even until piece measures 20".

Joining Pieces

Beg with back, sk first 4 sts, sc until 4 sts rem; sk 4 sts on first sleeve and sc until 4 sts rem; sk 4 sts on front and sc until 4 sts rem; sk 4 sts on second sleeve and sc until 4 sts rem = 176 (200, 224) sts; turn and ch 1. Sc across all sts; turn and ch 1. Place a removable marker at each of the 3 raglan seams and then cont. working back and forth.

Raglan Shaping

Row 1: Work 1 sc, sc2tog, *sc to 3 sts before next seam, sc2tog, 2 sc, sc2tog*; rep from * to * 2 more times, sc until 3 sts rem, sc2tog, 1 sc (8-st dec).

Row 2: Work in sc without dec.

Rep rows 1 and 2 until 104 sts rem.

Collar

Change to 6 mm hook and work even for 1½". Change to 7 mm hook and work even until collar measures 7".

Finishing

Sew raglan and collar seams. Sew side and sleeve seams. Join the 8 sts at each side of the underarms. Weave in ends.

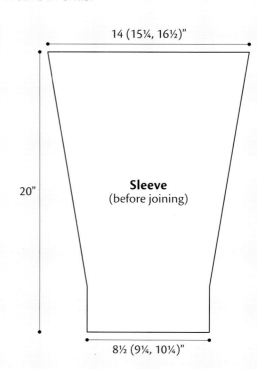

14 (15¼, 16½)"

20"

Sleeve
(before joining)

8½ (9¼, 10¼)"

16 (16, 17)"

Back/Front
(before joining)

17¾ (20¼, 22¾)"

SIDE-TO-SIDE SWEATER

This unique sweater is made in front-post double crochet, which gives the appearance of a knitted fabric. Its side-to-side construction adds to the knitted look.

Finished Measurements

Bust: 31 (36, 41)"

Length: 20¼ (21, 21½)"

Materials

500 (600, 700) g; 2,734 (3,280; 3,825) yds of fine-weight baby alpaca **2**

4 mm crochet hook

Gauge

23 sts and 24 rows = 4" (unstretched)

Front-Post Double Crochet (FPdc) Pattern

Work front-post double crochet (FPdc) around every dc post on previous row. Turn and ch 1 at end of every row.

Back

The sweater is worked from side to side, beg at side seam.

Ch 81 (81, 83). Dc in 2nd ch from hook and in each ch across = 80 (80, 82) dc.

Starting on RS row, work in FPdc until there are 6 (7, 7) ridges on RS of work, approx 2 (2¼, 2½)". Ch 37 (41, 43) new sts on one end for shoulder. Dc in 2nd ch from hook and across next 35 (39, 41) dc, work in FPdc across rem sts = 116 (120, 124) sts.

Work even in patt until piece measures 13½ (15¾, 18)".

Bind off by working sl st across 36 (40, 42) sts for shoulder.

Work even in patt until piece measures 15½ (18, 20½)".

Front

Ch 81 (81, 83). Dc in 2nd ch from hook and in each ch across = 80 (80, 82) dc.

Starting on a RS row, work in FPdc until there are 6 (6, 7) ridges on RS of work, approx 2 (2¼, 2½)". Ch 37 (41, 43) new sts on one end for shoulder. Dc in 2nd ch from hook and across next 35 (39, 41) dc, work in FPdc across rem sts = 116 (120, 124) sts.

Work until piece measures 5½ (6½, 7¾)" from beg or 3½ (4¼, 5¼)" from shoulder seam.

Ch 15 (15, 17) new sts for collar, dc in 2nd ch from hook and in next 13 (13, 15) sts, work FPdc across rem sts = 130 (134, 140) sts.

Work even in patt until piece measures 7¾ (8¾, 10¼)" from side seam; collar should measure approx 2¼ (2½, 2½)".

V-neck: Beg at lower edge, dc 60 (64, 69), ch 71 (71, 72) new sts. Dc in 2nd ch from hook and in next 69 (69, 70) sts, work in patt across rem sts = 130 (134, 140) sts.

Work even in patt until piece measures 2¼ (2½, 2½)".

Sl 14 (14, 16) sts to end collar = 116 (120, 124) sts.

Work even in patt for 3½ (4¼, 5¼)".

Sl 36 (40, 42) sts to end shoulder = 80 (80, 82) sts.

Work even in patt for 2 (2¼, 2½)" or until piece measures 15½ (18, 20½)" from side seam.

Sleeves

Inc for sleeve length on one end, and for sleeve cap on the other end.

Ch 29. Dc in 2nd ch from hook and in each ch across = 28 sts.

Work 1 row in patt and then ch 11 new sts. *Dc in 2nd ch from hook and in next 9 chs, work in patt across rem dc, ch 1 new st, turn and ch 1. Work 1 dc in new st and in patt for rem of row, ch 11 new sts*. Rep from * to * until 40 sts have been increased for sleeve length and 3 sts have been increased for sleeve cap = 71 sts total.

Cont in patt, but ch 2 new sts for sleeve cap until there are 95 sts total. Ch 21 for sleeve length (for wrist), and cont inc 2 ch sts for sleeve cap until there are a total of 119 sts.

Now work only the inc for sleeve cap; ch 3 new sts twice = 125 sts.

Work even until there are 17 (19, 21) ridges at widest point = 5½ (6¼, 6¾)".

Beg dec and work sl sts where you had previously increased with ch sts until 28 sts rem.

Finishing

Join ends of collar at center back and sew collar down along back neck. Sew shoulder seams. Sew side seams. Attach sleeves, fitting sleeve cap into armhole. Sew sleeve seams except for the top 2 (2¼, 2¼)", which are joined to the slipped sts at underarm on body of sweater. Weave in ends.

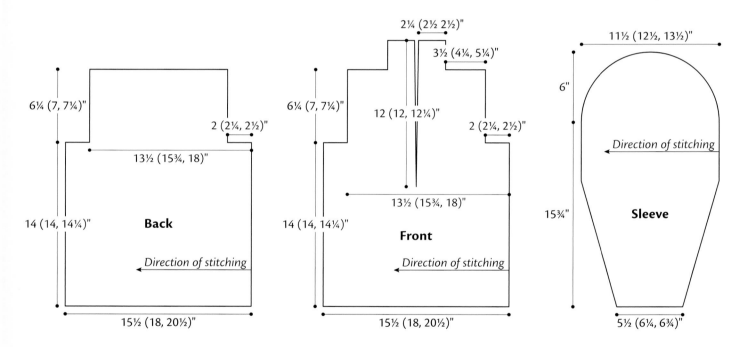

Back

6¼ (7, 7¼)"
2 (2¼, 2½)"
13½ (15¾, 18)"
14 (14, 14¼)"
Direction of stitching
15½ (18, 20½)"

Front

2¼ (2½ 2½)"
3½ (4¼, 5¼)"
6¼ (7, 7¼)"
12 (12, 12¼)"
2 (2¼, 2½)"
13½ (15¾, 18)"
14 (14, 14¼)"
Direction of stitching
15½ (18, 20½)"

Sleeve

11½ (12½, 13½)"
6"
15¾"
Direction of stitching
5½ (6¼, 6¾)"

Keep the chill away with this wear-anywhere jacket. The shaping is a bit challenging but worth the attention required.

Finished Measurements

Bust: 37 (42¼, 46¼, 50)" without overlapping front edges

Length: 23 (24, 24, 25)"

Materials

650 (700, 750, 900) g; 1,202 (1,312; 1,422; 1,640) yds of bulky-weight wool or wool/acrylic blend 5

6 mm crochet hook

Removable stitch marker

Gauge

11 sts and 10 rows = 4" in patt

Stitch Pattern

Row 1: *Insert hook through st, yarn around hook, and pull through; yarn around hook, insert hook through the same st, yarn around hook, and pull through; yarn around hook and pull hook through the 4 loops on hook = 1 patt group; ch 1, sk 1 st*. Rep from * to * across, ending with 1 sc in last st; turn and ch 1.

Row 2: Work as for row 1, but work into ch sp between patt groups, starting with a sc into first st of row and then a ch-1, and ending with 1 patt group and then a sc.

Rep row 2 throughout.

Back

At end of every row, turn and ch 1.

Ch 51 (57, 61, 63). Sc in 2nd ch from hook and in each ch across = 50 (56, 60, 62) sc.

Work 4 rows in sc.

Change to patt and work until piece measures 23 (24, 24, 25)".

Left Front

Ch 27 (31, 35, 39). Sc in 2nd ch from hook and in each ch across = 26 (30, 34, 38) sc.

Work 4 rows in sc.

Work in patt and sc edge as follows:

Row 1: Work 4 sc, then in patt over rem 22 (26, 30, 34) sts.

Row 2: Work until 4 sts rem, sk 1 st, work 3 sc.

Rep rows 1 and 2 until piece measures 9 (9½, 9½, 10)".

Beg on next row and then on every 4th row, work 1 more st in sc at front edge and 1 less st in patt until there are 10 (12, 12, 14) sc, and then on every other row until there are 12 (14, 16, 18) sc at front edge and 14 (16, 18, 20) sts in patt.

Work even until piece measures 23 (24, 24, 25)".

Right Front

Work as for left front, but reverse sc edge as follows:

Row 1: Work 22 (26, 30, 34) sts in patt, sk 1 st, 3 sc; turn and ch 1.

Row 2: Work 4 sc, then in patt over rem 22 (26, 30, 34) sts; turn and ch 1.

Sleeves

Ch 25 (27, 29, 29); turn and ch 1. Sc in 2nd ch from hook and in each ch across = 24 (26, 28, 28) sc.

Work 4 rows in sc.

Change to patt and, on next row, inc 1 st at each side as follows: 1 sc, 2 sc in next st, work to last 2 sts, 2 sc in next st, 1 sc. Rep inc on every 4th row until there are 44 (46, 48, 52) sts.

Work even until sleeve measures 20".

Finishing

Join shoulder seams. Attach sleeves to jacket. Sew sleeve and side seams.

Hood: Beg at right front edge, sc 12 (14, 16, 18) sts on right front, 26 (24, 20, 22) sts along back neck, 12 (14, 16, 18) sts on left front = 50 (52, 52, 58) sts. Place marker at center back. Working back and forth, inc 1 st by working 2 sc in st with marker on every other row 8 times = 58 (60, 60, 66) sts. Work even until hood measures 9". Sc2tog on each side of marker on every other row 3 times. Cut yarn and sew hood tog at top.

Weave in ends.

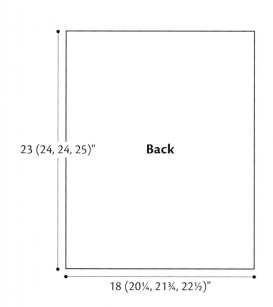

23 (24, 24, 25)" — **Back**

18 (20¼, 21¾, 22½)"

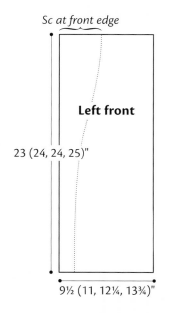

Sc at front edge

Left front

23 (24, 24, 25)"

9½ (11, 12¼, 13¾)"

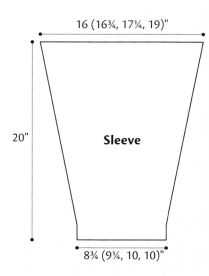

16 (16¾, 17¼, 19)"

20" — **Sleeve**

8¾ (9¼, 10, 10)"

V-NECK DRESS

If you've ever thought of crocheting a dress, this is the one. It's easy to make in double crochet and comfortable to wear.

Finished Measurements

Bust: 28 (32, 36, 39½)"
Length: 37 (38, 39½, 42¼)"

Materials

300 (350, 400, 450) g; 1,640 (1,914; 2,186; 2,460) yds of fine-weight baby alpaca 2
4 mm crochet hook
Removable stitch markers

Gauge

19 sts and 10 rows = 4" in dc

Front

At end of every row, turn and ch 2.

Ch 102 (112, 122, 130); turn and ch 2. Dc in 3rd ch from hook and in each ch across = 100 (110, 120, 128) dc.

Dec: On next row, dec 1 st at each side as follows: work 1 dc, dc2tog, dc to last 3 sts, dc2tog, 1 dc. Rep dec on every 4th row until 66 (76, 86, 94) sts rem.

Work even in dc until piece measures 28¾".

Back

Work as for front.

V-neck and raglan seams: Beg at center neck, work 1 dc, dc2tog, *dc to 3 sts before next seam, dc2tog, 2 dc, dc2tog*; rep from * to * 3 more times and, when 3 sts rem, dc2tog, work 1 dc (8-st dec for raglan and 1-st dec at each side of V-neck). Work dec for raglan on every row. Work dec for V-neck on every other row 9 (7, 6, 6) times and then on every row until no more sts rem for front = 48 (54, 56, 58) sts.

Finishing

Sew side and sleeve seams. Join the 10 (10, 10, 14) sts on each side of the underarms. Weave in ends.

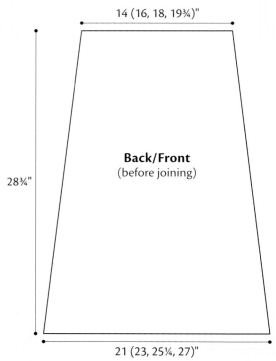

14 (16, 18, 19¾)"

Back/Front
(before joining)

28¾"

21 (23, 25¼, 27)"

Sleeves

Ch 42 (44, 46, 48). Dc in 3rd ch from hook and in each dc across = 40 (42, 44, 46) dc.

Inc: On next row, inc 1 st at each side as follows: work 1 dc, 2 dc in next st, dc to last 2 sts, 2 dc in next st, 1 dc. Rep inc every 3rd row until there are 60 (64, 66, 72) sts.

Work even in dc until sleeve measures 12¾ (13½, 13½, 13½)".

Joining Pieces

Join the front, back, and sleeves to complete the V neck and the raglan seams.

Mark center front with removable marker at st 33 (38, 43, 47). Join new yarn at marker, work across rem part of row in dc until 5 (5, 5, 7) sts rem; sk first 5 (5, 5, 7) sts of sleeve and work in dc until 5 (5, 5, 7) sts rem; sk first 5 (5, 5, 7) sts of back and work in dc until 5 (5, 5, 7) sts rem; sk 5 (5, 5, 7) sts of second sleeve and work in dc until 5 (5, 5, 7) sts rem; sk 5 (5, 5, 7) sts on other side of front and work in dc to center front = 212 (240, 264, 276) dc. Turn and ch 2. Place removable marker at each of the 4 raglan seams, and work back and forth as follows:

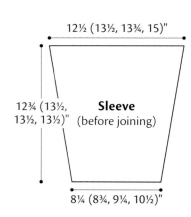

12½ (13½, 13¾, 15)"

12¾ (13½, 13½, 13½)"

Sleeve
(before joining)

8¼ (8¾, 9¼, 10½)"

HOODED CAPE

*Keep yourself warm on any outing in this easy-to-make
cape and hood. It's worked in double crochet
with shoulder seams for a flattering fit.*

Finished Measurements

Hem circumference: 49½ (54, 59)"

Length to beg of hood: 17 (18½, 18½)"

Materials

250 (350, 434) g; 875 (1,312; 1,530) yds of light worsted–weight alpaca ⟨③⟩

3 mm and 4 mm crochet hooks

Removable stitch markers

Gauge

17 sts and 10 rows = 4" with 4 mm hook

Back and Front

Cape is worked in one piece from the bottom to the beginning of the neck shaping and shoulder seams.

At end of every row, turn and ch 2.

With 4 mm hook, ch 212 (232, 252). Dc in 3rd ch from hook and in each ch across = 210 (230, 250) dc.

Work in dc until piece measures 10¼ (11¼, 11¼)". Place a marker 60 (65, 70) sts from each side for side seams.

Neck and Shoulder Shaping

Work back and forth across each piece as follows:

Right front: Work back and forth over right front sts only. For dec at front edge, sl 1 st on every other row a total of 10 times (10 sts dec at front edge). For dec at side seam, shape shoulder by working to required number of sts to dec, then turn and work back to front edge. On every other row, dec 1 st 3 times; then on every row, dec 1 st 5 times, 2 sts 4 (4, 5) times, 3 sts 2 (2, 3) times, and 5 sts 0 (1, 1) time. You should end with 28 sts (dec are worked over a total of 17 (18, 20) rows). Work even at side seam on Small and Medium until front edge decs are finished.

Back: Work dec at beg and end of row as follows: Work sl sts across required number of sts at beg of row and work to required number of sts to dec at end of row, then turn and work back. At each side, dec 1 st every other row 3 times. Then on every row, dec 1 st 5 times, 2 sts 4 (4, 5) times, 3 sts 2 (2, 3) times, and 5 sts 0 (1, 1)) time. You should end with 46 sts (dec are worked over a total of 17 (18, 20) rows. Work even on Small and Medium until back is same length as front.

Left front: Work as for right front, reversing shaping. For side-seam dec, sl st across required number of sts. For front-edge dec, work to last st and turn.

Finishing

Join shoulder seams.

Hood: Dc across right front, back neck, and left front = 102 dc. Work even for 10¼". Sew tog from center back to front edges. With 3 mm hook, work 1 row of sc along front edge of hood. Weave in ends.

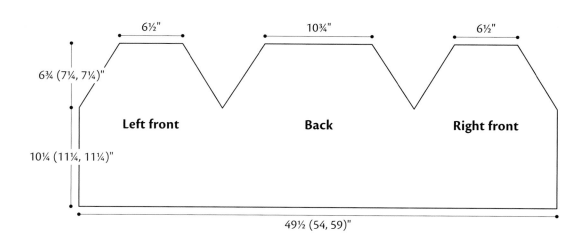

SHAWL-COLLARED JACKET

The shawl collar makes this jacket special. The stitch pattern—for crocheters with some experience— makes the collar stand straight up at the back neck.

Finished Measurements

Bust: 35½ (41½, 46)"

Length: 19 (21, 22)"

Materials

700 (800, 950) g; 1,202 (1,312, 1,550) yds of bulky-weight wool and acrylic blend **(5)**

6 mm crochet hook

Gauge

13 sts and 13 rows = 4" in st patt

Stitch Pattern

Back-Post Single Crochet: Work sc into the little loop under the chain-link loop as follows: Insert hook from below and then up in the little loop, which lies horizontally under the st, and complete sc. Rep across the row in every st; turn and ch 1.

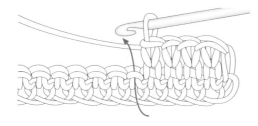

Rep for every row.

Back

At end of all rows, turn and ch 1.

Ch 55 (65, 73). Sc in 2nd ch from hook and in each ch across = 54 (64, 72) sc.

Work in st patt until piece measures 19 (21, 22)".

Left Front

Ch 32 (37, 40). Sc in 2nd ch from hook and in each ch across = 31 (36, 39) sc.

Work in st patt until piece measures 19 (21, 22)".

Collar: Sl st 16 (20, 23) sts for shoulders, work collar in patt over rem 15 (16, 16) sts for 3½ (4, 4½)".

Right Front

Work as for left front, reversing shaping.

Sleeves

Ch 31 (33, 35). Sc in 2nd ch from hook and in each ch across = 30 (32, 34) sts.

Work in st patt until sleeve measures 3¼".

Inc: On next row, inc 1 st at each side as follows: work 1 sc, 2 sc in next st, work to last 2 sts, 2 sc in next st, 1 sc. Rep inc every 5 (5, 4) rows until there are 46 (48, 56) sts.

Cont even in st patt until sleeve measures 18 (19, 19)".

Sleeve cap: Sl 2 sts, work to last 2 sts, turn, ch 1. Work 1 row even. Dec on every other row 2 times as follows: work 1 sc, sc2tog, work to last 3 sts, sc2tog, 1 sc. Work 1 row even = 38 (40, 48) sts rem.

Finishing

Join shoulder seams. Sew ends of collar tog at center back and sew down to back neck. Attach sleeves and sew sleeve and side seams. Weave in ends.

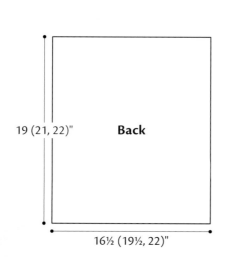

19 (21, 22)" **Back**

16½ (19½, 22)"

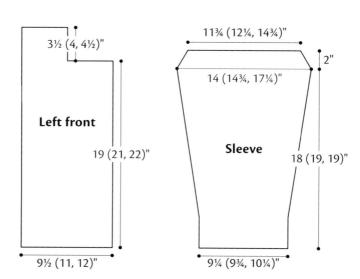

3½ (4, 4½)"

Left front

19 (21, 22)"

9½ (11, 12)"

11¾ (12¼, 14¾)"

2"

14 (14¾, 17¼)"

Sleeve

18 (19, 19)"

9¼ (9¾, 10¼)"

TUNISIAN JACKET

This stylish jacket is worked using Tunisian (or afghan) crochet, which is simple to master. You'll need an afghan crochet hook to work this.

Finished Measurements

Bust: 37 (41½, 46½)" without overlap
Length: 20½ (21½, 22½)"

Materials

800 (900; 1,000) g; 1,312 (1,422; 1,640) yds of bulky-weight wool/acrylic/nylon blend ⑤

6 mm afghan crochet hook

Gauge

14 sts and 26 rows = 4"

Back

Ch 63 (70, 81).

Work in Tunisian crochet (see page 86) until piece measures 3¼ (3¼, 3½)", ending with a completed return row.

Dec: On next row, dec 1 st at each side as follows: work 1 sc, sc2tog, work to last 3 sts, sc2tog, 1 sc. Rep dec on every 3rd row 2 more times = 57 (64, 75) sts rem.

Work until piece measures 8 (8½, 9)", ending with a completed return row.

Inc: On next row, inc 1 st at each side by working 2 sts in first and last st. Rep inc on every 5th row 2 more times = 63 (70, 81) sts.

Work even until piece measures 13 (13½, 14)", ending with a completed return row.

Armholes: Sl 5 sts, work to last 5 sts, leave rem sts unworked = 53 (60, 71) sts.

Work even until piece measures 20½ (21½, 22½)".

Left Front

Ch 33 (38, 41).

Work as for back to armhole, but work shaping only on right-hand side as seen from RS, ending with a completed return row.

Armhole: Sl 5 sts, work to end of row = 28 (32, 36) sts.

Work even until piece measures 20½ (21½, 22½)", ending with a completed return row.

Collar: Sl 16 (20, 22) sts for shoulder, then work collar over rem 12 (12, 14) sts for 3¼ (3½, 4)".

Right Front

Work as for left front, reversing shaping as follows: For armhole, work to last 5 sts and leave those sts unworked. Work collar on first 12 (12, 14) sts for 3¼ (3½, 4)", leaving rem sts for shoulder unworked.

Sleeves

Ch 33 (37, 37).

Work in Tunisian crochet until sleeve measures 3¼", ending with a completed return row.

Inc: On next row, inc 1 st at each side as follows: work 1 sc, 2 sc in next st, work to last 2 sts, 2 sc in next st, 1 sc. Rep inc every 8 (8, 9) rows until there are 50 (55, 57) sts.

Work even until piece measures 21", ending with a completed return row.

Sleeve cap: On next row, sl 4 sts, work to last 4 sts, and leave rem sts unworked. Rep dec 2 more times = 27 (31, 33) sts rem.

Finishing

Join shoulder seams. Join collar ends at center back and then sew collar down along back neck. Attach sleeves. Sew side seams. Sew sleeve seams to 1½" from underarm, then sew sleeves to jacket at underarms.

Steam the edges to prevent rolling. Weave in ends.

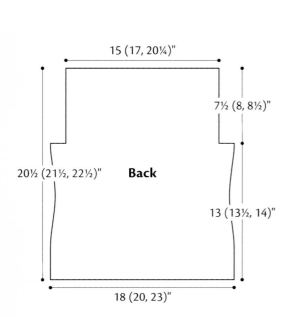

Back

15 (17, 20¼)"
7½ (8, 8½)"
20½ (21½, 22½)"
13 (13½, 14)"
18 (20, 23)"

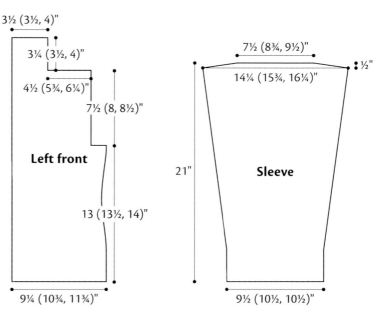

Left front

3½ (3½, 4)"
3¼ (3½, 4)"
4½ (5¾, 6¼)"
7½ (8, 8½)"
13 (13½, 14)"
9¼ (10¾, 11¾)"

Sleeve

7½ (8¾, 9½)"
½"
14¼ (15¾, 16¼)"
21"
9½ (10½, 10½)"

This stitch is also known as afghan stitch. The right side is always facing and the piece is not turned from row to row, except after the initial chain stitches.

Chain the exact number of sts you need.

Row 1 (starting row, worked from right to left): Insert the hook into the top loop of the second chain from the hook, yarn around hook, and pull through chain; leave the loop on the hook (2 loops on hook). *Insert the hook into the next chain, yarn around hook, and pull through a loop. Repeat from * for each chain stitch across, keeping all loops on the hook. Do not turn the work.

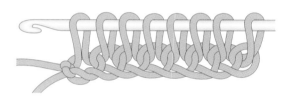

Row 2 (return row, worked from left to right): With the right side still facing you, yarn around hook and pull through 1 loop. This counts as the turning chain for the next row.

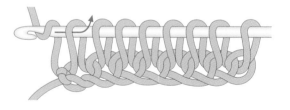

*Yarn around hook and pull through 2 loops. Repeat from * across the row until 1 loop remains on the hook.

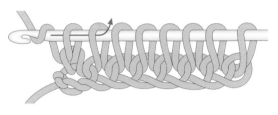

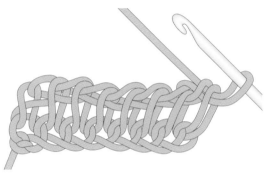

Note that there are no turning stitches, so work edge stitches loosely.

Row 3 (forward row, worked from right to left): Insert the hook under the first vertical thread of a stitch (do not work into the vertical thread below the first loop on your hook), yarn around hook, and pull through a loop. Repeat across the row, keeping all loops on the hook, to the last vertical thread.

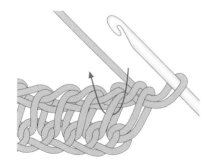

Insert the hook under both vertical threads at the end, yarn around hook, and pull through a loop.

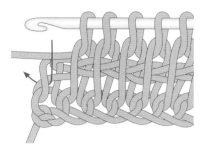

Rep rows 2 and 3.

Increase (inc 1 st): Insert the hook under the strand that lies behind the two horizontal threads that are between two vertical threads, yarn over hook, and pull through a loop, giving you an extra loop on the hook. This increase is worked the same at either end of the row. On the next row, the extra loop is treated as a normal stitch.

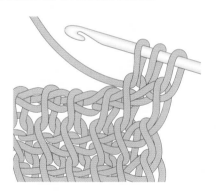

Decrease (dec 1 st): Insert the hook through 2 vertical loops on the forward row, yarn around hook, and pull through both vertical threads; keep the loop on the hook. This decrease is worked the same at either end of a row.

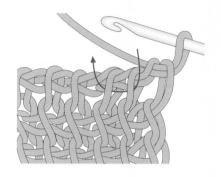

Armhole shaping: To shape armholes, you will slip a stitch at the beginning of a forward row and stop stitching at the required spot at the end of the row. To work a slip stitch at the beginning of the row, insert the hook into the second vertical stitch, yarn around hook, and draw through 2 loops.

Continue until the required number of stitches is bound off. Then work across the row and leave the required number of stitches unworked. Work the next row as a normal return row.

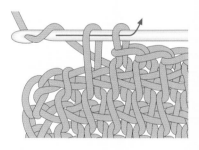

COAT
WITH SHAWL COLLAR

This long coat will keep you in style through fall, winter, and spring. It's worked in one piece to the armholes. Then the fronts and back are worked separately, and the shawl collar is added at the end.

Finished Measurements

Bust: 32 (34½, 37½)"

Length: 33 (34, 35)"

Note that coat will stretch in length and width.

Materials

1,000 (1,100; 1,200) g; 656 (722, 786) yds of super bulky–weight wool/acrylic/alpaca blend (6)

10 mm and 15 mm crochet hooks

Optional: 4 or 5 large buttons, 1½" to 2" in diameter

Gauge

6 sts and 3.5 rows = 4" in dc using larger hook

Back and Fronts

Back and fronts are worked in one piece to armholes.

With 15 mm hook, ch 57 (61, 65). Sc in 2nd ch from hook and in each ch across = 56 (60, 64) sc; turn and ch 1. Work 2 more rows in sc.

Change to dc and turn every row with ch 2 (counts as 1 dc).

Work in dc for 6 (7, 7)".

Dec: Dec on every other row as follows:

1st dec row: Work 13 (14, 15) dc, dc2tog, 26 (28, 30) dc, dc2tog, 13 (14, 15) dc.

2nd dec row: Work 13 (14, 15) dc, dc2tog, 24 (26, 28) dc, dc2tog, 13 (14, 15) dc.

3rd dec row: Work 12 (13, 14) dc, dc2tog, 24 (26, 28) dc, dc2tog, 12 (13, 14) dc.

4th dec row: Work 12 (13, 14) dc, dc2tog, 22 (24, 26) dc, dc2tog, 12 (13, 14) dc.

5th dec row: Work 11 (12, 13) dc, dc2tog, 22 (24, 26) dc, dc2tog, 11 (12, 13) dc.

6th dec row: Work 11 (12, 13) dc, dc2tog, 20 (22, 24) dc, dc2tog, 11 (12, 13) dc = 44 (48, 52) sts.

Work 3 rows even.

Inc: Inc on every other row as follows:

1st inc row: Work 11 (12, 13) dc, 2 dc in next st, 20 (22, 24) dc, 2 dc in next st, 11 (12, 13) dc.

2nd inc row: Work 11 (12, 13) dc, 2 dc in next st, 22 (24, 26) dc, 2 dc in next st, 11 (12, 13) dc = 48 (52, 56) sts.

Neck and Armholes

Work each piece separately as follows:

Right front: Work 1 dc, dc2tog, 7 (8, 9) dc; turn and cont in dc, dec 1 st at front edge on every row until 5 (6, 7) sts rem. Work 1 (1, 2) rows for shoulder.

Back: Sk 4 sts for underarm and work 20 (22, 24) dc. Work even until back is same length as front; on last row, work 5 (6, 7) dc, 10 (10, 10) sc, 5 (6, 7) dc.

Left front: Skip 4 sts for underarm and work 7 (8, 9) dc, dc2tog, 1 dc. Work as for right front, but reverse shaping.

Sleeves

With 15 mm hook, ch 17. Sc in 2nd ch from hook and in each ch across = 16 sc. Turn and ch 1.

Work 7 more rows of sc.

Inc: Change to dc, inc 1 st at each side as follows: 1 dc, 2 dc in next st, dc to last 2 sts, 2 dc in next st, 1 dc. Work inc on every 3rd row until there are 20 (20, 22) sts.

Work even until sleeve measures 19½".

Finishing

Join shoulders. Sew sleeve seams to top ¾" to 1¼", and join to 4 sts at underarm.

Collar: Working in sc with 15 mm hook and beg at back neck at sc row, work 10 sc; turn and work back, working 3 more sts on next dc row along neck. Cont in this way, with 3 more sts at each side until you've reached the starting point for V-neck.

Front bands: Do not cut yarn, but change to 10 mm hook and work 1 row of sc along front edges; turn and work back to collar; change to 15 mm hook and sc along collar. Change back to 10 mm hook and work 1 row of sc along front edge; turn and work back to collar. Cut yarn and weave in tail on WS.

If desired, sew buttons on left front, placing first one at collar and the rest evenly spaced about 4" apart. Use stitches on right front as buttonholes.

Weave in ends.

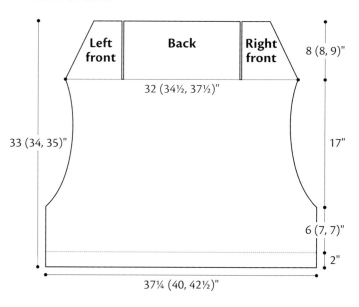

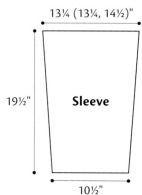

CROCHET BASICS

Below you'll find a brief explanation for the simple crochet stitches required to make the projects in this book.

Chain (ch)

Chain stitches are used for casting on and turning. Make a slipknot over the hook.

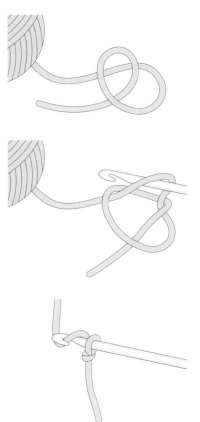

Insert the hook through the loop and tighten yarn slightly. Wrap yarn around the hook and bring it through the loop. Continue bringing the yarn through each loop until the chain has the desired number of stitches. Do not count the loop of the slip stitch.

Single Crochet (sc)

Insert hook into chain or stitch, wrap yarn around hook, and pull through stitch; wrap yarn around hook and pull through two loops on hook.

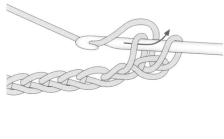

Continue in this way across the row. Turn and chain 1.

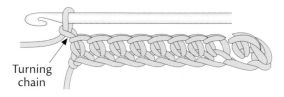

Turning chain

The next row begins in the first stitch after the turning chain (see page 92) and ends on the last stitch. Make sure the stitch count across the row is accurate.

90

Double Crochet (dc)

Wrap yarn around hook and insert hook into specified chain or stitch.

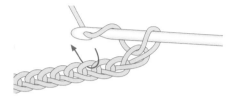

Wrap yarn around hook and pull through stitch; (wrap yarn around hook and pull hook through 2 loops on hook) twice. Continue in this way across the row. Turn and chain 3.

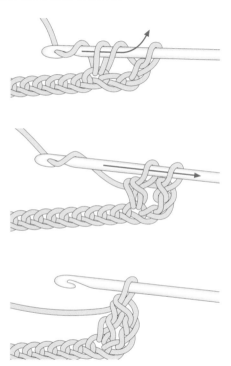

The next row begins in the stitch next to the one below the turning chain and ends with a stitch in the top of the turning chain, unless otherwise instructed.

Treble Crochet (tr)

Wrap yarn around hook twice and insert hook into specified chain or stitch.

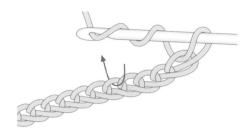

Wrap yarn around hook and pull through stitch; (wrap yarn around and pull hook through 2 loops on hook) 3 times. Continue in this way across the row. Turn and chain 4.

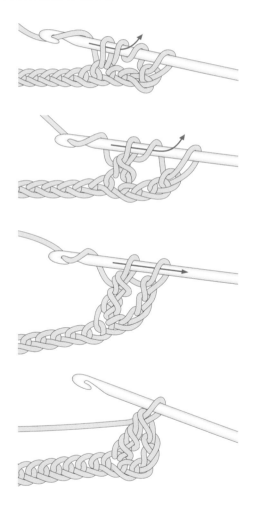

Slip Stitch (sl st)

Insert hook into chain or stitch, wrap yarn around hook, and pull through both loops on hook.

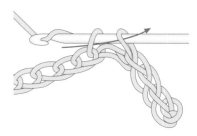

Join into a Ring

Make the required number of chain stitches. Insert hook through the first chain made. Wrap yarn around hook and pull through stitch.

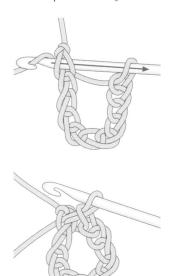

Turning Chains

Turning chains are stitches made at the beginning of every new row or round so that the sides of the piece will be the same height as the stitches across the row. If you are working around in a spiral, the turning stitches will torque slightly.

Gauge

Gauge, which is specified in each pattern, should be tested with a swatch that you crochet beforehand. Make the swatch about 6" x 6". Measure a 4" x 4" portion and count the number of stitches and rows. If the gauge isn't correct, you'll need to try again with a smaller or larger hook. If there are too many stitches, try a bigger hook; if there are too few stitches, use a smaller size hook.

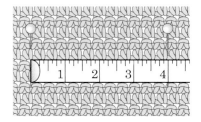

Ball bands on yarn list the size of knitting needles suitable for that yarn. However, they don't list crochet-hook sizes. To start, try a crochet hook equivalent to the knitting-needle size; metric equivalents are most useful for this.

Decreasing with Single Crochet (sc2tog)

(Insert hook into next stitch, wrap yarn around hook, pull through stitch) twice; wrap yarn around hook, and pull through all 3 loops on hook— 1 stitch decreased.

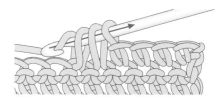

Increasing with Single Crochet (2 sc in next st)

Work 2 stitches into the same stitch—1 stitch increased.

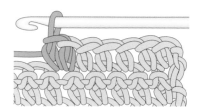

Finishing

There are several methods for joining pieces of crochet.

Shoulder Seams with Tapestry Needle

With right sides facing up and pieces aligned, insert the needle into the first chain on the top piece at the beginning of the row and out the next chain. Then insert the needle into the corresponding chain on the bottom piece and out the next chain. Repeat until seam is completed. Weave in ends.

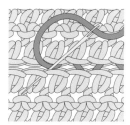

Side Seams with Tapestry Needle

With right sides facing up and pieces next to each other, insert the needle under one stitch at the edge on one side, then under the corresponding stitch at the edge on the other side. Continue working from one side to the other, inserting the needle in the spot where you came out the previous time. Repeat until seam is completed. Weave in ends.

Single-Crochet Seams

With right sides of pieces facing each other, insert hook under stitch on the front piece and then into corresponding stitch on the back piece, wrap yarn around hook, and work single crochet stitch. Repeat until seam is completed. Weave in ends.

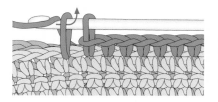

Slip-Stitch Seams

With right sides of pieces facing each other, insert hook under stitch on front piece and then into corresponding stitch on back piece, wrap yarn around hook, and pull yarn through the stitch and the loop on the hook. Repeat until seam is completed. Weave in ends.

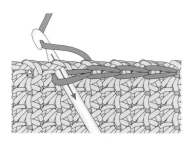

Zippers

Plastic separating zippers come in a variety of sizes and colors. If you can't find the exact size needed, you can easily shorten a longer zipper to fit. To shorten, tightly whipstitch across the zipper teeth 8 to 10 times, just above where you want the zipper to end. Cut the zipper about ½" above the stitches. Hand sew the zipper in place with a needle and sewing thread.

Variations

The surface appearance of the crochet can differ, depending on which loop of the stitch you crochet into. Normally stitches are worked into both loops of the stitch on the row below. If you crochet into the front loops, ridges appear on the back. If you crochet into the back loops, ridges appear on the front.

Front loop   Back loop   Both loops

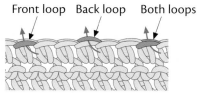

USEFUL INFORMATION

Standard Yarn-Weight System

Yarn-Weight Symbol and Category Name	0 LACE	1 SUPER FINE	2 FINE	3 LIGHT	4 MEDIUM	5 BULKY	6 SUPER BULKY
Types of Yarn in Category	Fingering 10-count crochet thread	Sock, Fingering, Baby	Sport, Baby	DK, Light worsted	Worsted, Afghan, Aran	Chunky, Craft, Rug	Bulky, Roving
Crochet Gauge* Ranges in Single Crochet in 4"	32 to 42** sts	21 to 32 sts	16 to 20 sts	12 to 17 sts	11 to 14 sts	8 to 11 sts	5 to 9 sts
Recommended Hook in Metric Size Range	Regular hook 2.25 mm	2.25 to 3.5 mm	3.5 to 4.5 mm	4.5 to 5.5 mm	5.5 to 6.5 mm	6.5 to 9 mm	9 mm and larger
Recommended Needle in U.S. Size Range	Regular hook B-1	B-1 to E-4	E-4 to 7	7 to I-9	I-9 to K-10½	K-10½ to M13	M-13 and larger

*These are guidelines only. The above reflect the most commonly used gauges and hook sizes for specific yarn categories.

**Lace-weight yarns are usually knit or crocheted on larger needles and hooks to create lacy, openwork patterns, so a gauge range is difficult to determine. Always follow the gauge stated in your pattern.

Crochet Hook Sizes

Millimeter	U.S. Size*
2.25 mm	B-1
2.75 mm	C-2
3.25 mm	D-3
3.5 mm	E-4
3.75 mm	F-5
4 mm	G-6
4.5 mm	7
5 mm	H-8
5.5 mm	I-9

Millimeter	U.S. Size*
6 mm	J-10
6.5 mm	K-10½
8 mm	L-11
9 mm	M/N-13
10 mm	N/P-15
12 mm	O
15 mm	P/Q
16 mm	Q
19 mm	S

*U.S. sizes may vary by manufacturer. It's best to select hooks based on metric (millimeter) sizes.

Metric Conversions

m = yds x 0.9144
yds = m x 1.0936
g = oz x 28.35
oz = g x 0.0352